THE NATIONAL SOCIETY FOR PERFORMANCE AND INSTRUCTION (NSPI)

The National Society for Performance and Instruction (NSPI) is the leading international association dedicated to improving productivity and performance in the workplace. Founded in 1962, NSPI represents over ten thousand members throughout the United States and Canada and in thirty-three other countries. NSPI members work in over three thousand businesses, governmental agencies, academic institutions, and other organizations. Monthly meetings of over sixty different chapters provide professional development, services, and information exchange.

NSPI members include performance technologists, training directors, human resource managers, instructional technologists, human factors practitioners, and organizational development consultants. They are business executives, professors, line managers, government leaders, and military commanders. They work in a variety of areas: the armed forces, financial services, government agencies, health services, high technology, manufacturing, telecommunications, travel and hospitality, and universities. NSPI members are leaders in their fields and work settings. They are strategy-oriented, quality-focused, and results-centered.

The mission of NSPI is to improve the performance of individuals and organizations through the application of Human Performance Technology (HPT). NSPI's vision for itself is to be the preferred source of information, education, and advocacy for enhancing individual and organizational effectiveness, and to be respected for the tangible and enduring impact it is having on people, organizations, and the field of performance technology.

NSPI makes a difference to people by helping them grow into skilled professionals who use integrated and systematic approaches to add value to their organizations and the profession. Whether designing training programs, building selection or incentive systems, assisting organizations in their own redesign, or performing myriad other interventions, NSPI members produce results.

NSPI makes a difference to organizations by increasing professional competence and confidence. NSPI members help organizations anticipate opportunities and challenges and develop powerful solutions that contribute to productivity and satisfaction.

NSPI makes a difference to the field of performance technology by expanding the boundaries of what we know about defining, teaching, supporting, and maintaining skilled human performance. With a healthy respect for research and development, a variety of technologies, and collegial interaction, NSPI members use approaches and systems that ensure improved productivity and a better world.

For additional information, contact:

National Society for Performance and Instruction
1300 L Street, N.W., Suite 1250
Washington, DC 20005
Telephone: (202) 408-7969
Fax: (202) 408-7972

CREATING THE ERGONOMICALLY SOUND WORKPLACE

A PUBLICATION IN THE NSPI SERIES
From Training to Performance in the Twenty-First Century

CREATING THE ERGONOMICALLY SOUND WORKPLACE

Lee T. Ostrom

JOSSEY-BASS PUBLISHERS
SAN FRANCISCO

Substantial discounts on bulk quantities of Jossey-Bass books are available to corporations, professional associations, and other organizations. For details and discount information, contact the special sales department at Jossey-Bass Inc., Publishers. (415) 433-1740; Fax (415) 433-0499.

For sales outside the United States, contact Maxwell Macmillan International Publishing Group, 866 Third Avenue, New York, New York 10022.

Manufactured in the United States of America. Nearly all Jossey-Bass books and jackets are printed on recycled paper that contains at least 50 percent recycled waste, including 10 percent postconsumer waste. Many of our materials are also printed with vegetable-based ink; during the printing process these inks emit fewer volatile organic compounds (VOCs) than petroleum-based ink. VOCs contribute to the formation of smog.

Library of Congress Cataloging-in-Publication Data

Ostrom, Lee T.
    Creating the ergonomically sound workplace / Lee T. Ostrom.—1st ed.
      p.   cm.—(The Jossey-Bass management series)
    Includes bibliographical references and index.
    ISBN 1-55542-621-2
    1. Performance technology. 2. Office layout. 3. Human engineering. 4. Work environment. I. Title. II. Series.
HF5549.5.P37084   1994
658.2'3—dc20   93-41614
                                                    CIP

FIRST EDITION
PB Printing   *10 9 8 7 6 5 4 3 2 1*   *Code 9418*

CREATING THE ERGONOMICALLY SOUND WORKPLACE

CONTENTS

From Training to Performance in the Twenty-First Century: Introduction to the Book Series

For most trainers and instructional developers, the following request from a client sounds familiar: "I have a problem. Give me some training to solve it." We are taught to think that training is the answer to most human performance problems. But those of us who are veterans in the field have learned from our own experience and from others' research and theories that most of the problems our clients bring us are *not* best solved by training, or require some other solution in addition to training. What do we do in the face of this contradictory evidence?

We change our view of the world, our paradigm for thinking about how to solve our customers' problems. We look at practitioners in other fields and see how they recommend solving problems, and we try to incorporate their ideas and interventions into our own "bag of tricks."

We have heard and read about a wide array of such interventions: human-computer interface and workplace design; work process reengineering and sociotechnical systems; job aids, expert systems, and performance support systems; motivation, incentive, and feedback systems; organizational design, cultural change, and change management; measurement of results to demonstrate bottom-line savings. How do all these interventions fit together? Is there a field that incorporates and relates them? Yes. It is called Human Performance Technology (HPT).

What is human performance technology?

What makes HPT different from training, management consulting, and other practices aimed at improving the performance of people and organizations? According to Foshay and Moller (1992, p. 702), HPT is unique because it is "an applied field, not a discipline. It is structured primarily by the real world problem of human performance (in the workplace). It draws from any discipline that has prescriptive power in solving any human performance problem." Stolovitch and Keeps (1992, p.7) have incorporated a variety of definitions of the field into their descriptions of HPT's unique approach to synthesizing ideas borrowed from other disciplines:

HPT, therefore, is an engineering approach to attaining desired accomplishments from human performers. HP technologists are those who adopt a systems view of performance gaps, systematically analyze both gap and system, and design cost-effective and efficient interventions that are based on analysis data, scientific knowledge, and documented precedents, in order to close the gap in the most desirable manner.

Rummler and Brache (1992, p. 34) explain that the view HP technologists have of "what is going on . . . in organizations" is "fundamentally different" from views held by practitioners in other disciplines. HP technologists conceptualize "what is going on" by looking at and assessing three levels of variables that affect individual and organizational performance: the organization level, the work process level, and the job/worker level.

An HP technologist looks first at the total organization and at such variables as strategy and goals, structure, measurements, and management (see Figure P.1). Next, an HP technologist looks at work processes carried out across functions within the organization and analyzes the goals, design, measurement, and management of those processes to determine their effectiveness (see Figure P.2). Finally, an HP technologist looks at the job and the performer, focusing on five variables (Rummler and Brache, 1992, pp. 35–41):

1. *The performer.* Does the person have the physical, mental, and emotional ability as well as the skills and knowledge needed to perform?

2. *Inputs to the performer.* Are the available job procedures and work flow, information, money, tools, and the work environment adequate to support the desired performance?

3. *Outputs of the performer.* Do performance specifications for the outputs exist and is the performer aware of them?

4. *Consequences of the performer's actions.* Are consequences designed to support the performance and delivered in a timely manner?

5. *Feedback the performer receives about the performance.* Does the performer receive feedback, and if so, is it relevant, timely, accurate, and specific?

Figure P.3 illustrates the relationship between these principles.

Figure P.1. The Organization View of Work.

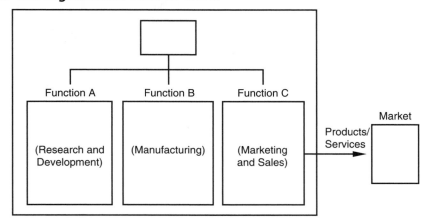

Source: Rummler and Brache, 1992, p. 35.

Figure P.2. The Cross-Functional View of Work Process.

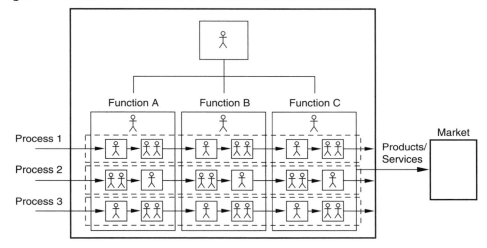

Source: Rummler and Brache, 1992, p. 37.

Figure P.3. The Job/Performer View of Work.

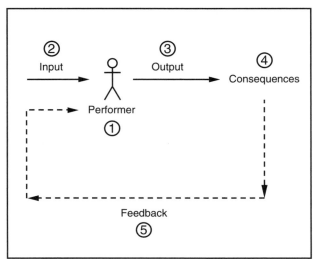

Source: Rummler and Brache, 1992, p. 38.

Purpose of the series
Once we have changed our worldview and accepted the notion of HPT interventions into our paradigm of how to approach the resolution of clients' problems, we would really like to try to implement some of them. But how?

1. Instruction is not the answer to every challenge in the workplace.

2. There are a wide array of interventions that can be used to enhance performance . . .

3. The HP technologist cannot be expected to be an expert in every intervention . . . [Rossett, 1992, p. 98].

As Rossett points out, it is not feasible for us to be experts in all these interventions. First, because the fields from which the interventions come are so diverse and constantly changing, it is virtually impossible for any of us to learn everything about and keep current in all fields. Second, there are very few resources out there to help us design and implement performance-enhancing interventions. Most books on the subject focus on what the inteventions are and why they are important, but contain precious few specific guidelines, procedures, or rules for how to actually carry out the interventions.

So, as practitioners we face several gaps: between our grounding in the "training" field and the recognition that we need to expand our worldview to include other performance-enhancing interventions; between our desire to learn about the other interventions and the difficulty of keeping current in all the fields from which they derive; and between the desire to try performance-enhancing interventions and the lack of specific, practical guidance on how to do so.

The series "From Training to Performance in the Twenty-First Century" tried to bridge these gaps. First, the series is based on two assumptions: (1) that training/instructional design/HPT practitioners are, for the most part, currently limited to implementing training interventions in the workplace, and (2) that most practitioners recognize the need to broaden their worldview and range of interventions to embrace the approach described above. The series is designed to serve as a bridge from training to other areas of HPT.

Second, the series is a *translation/how-to-do-it* series that tracks down and summarizes the knowledgebase of the fields from which the performance-enhancing interventions are derived and focuses on specific, practical *how-to* techniques for implementing performance-enhancing interventions in real job situations.

Organization of the series

To accomplish our purpose, we have organized the series into manageable chunks called Topics, each comprising three to five books that address a related set of performance-enhancing interventions. Each book covers one performance-enhancing intervention completely.

To implement the translation/how-to-do-it approach, maintain consistency across the series, and make the procedures as easy as possible to learn and use, each book makes extensive use of procedure and decision tables, forms, examples (both successful and unsuccessful), and case studies. Each book begins with a brief synthesis of the theoretical foundations of the intervention, acknowledging different points of view where they exist. This introductory material is followed by chapters containing a wide variety of procedures that show how to implement each intervention step by step. Many job aids and forms are provided. The book presents one or more real-world case studies showing the entire intervention in practice, complete with filled-out forms. It also provides a resource section that contains blank forms for reproduction. Finally, an extensive bibliography covers almost all the current thinking about the intervention.

Audience

The "From Training to Performance" series is designed for three audiences. The primary audience is trainers, training managers, and novice HPT practitioners, who will use the books as an on-the-job reference and work tool as they move from applying training solutions to using performance improvement interventions. The second audience is longtime instructional design and HPT practitioners, who will use the books for continuing education in performance improvement interventions that have evolved since they joined the field. The third audience is graduate students in training, instructional design, performance technology, organizational development, human resource development, and management, who will use the books to learn HPT techniques.

Each audience will use the series slightly differently. Trainers and training managers might want to begin with the case studies to see how the intervention really works, then go to the procedures and forms to try out the interventions. Graduate students will almost certainly begin with the theoretical material and integrate it into their schema of HPT before moving on to apply the procedures and forms to real-world or simulated performance problems. Veteran HPT practitioners might use either of the approaches, jumping back and forth between the procedures, case study and theory, or focusing on the design and usability of the procedures and forms that are of particular professional interest to them.

It is the fervent hope of the National Society for Performance and Instruction (NSPI) that readers will use the books in this series as a continuing source of self-development, training for others, and, most important, on-the-job reference tools, to provide clients with the most cost-effective and efficient interventions for solving their business problems.

Acknowledgments

This series would not exist without the help and support of the following people, who helped create and nurture it: the late Paul Tremper, NSPI's executive director from 1985 to 1993, who provided vision and emotional support for the series and expert handling of the seemingly infinite details associated with the series at NSPI; Maurice Coleman, vice president of research and development at NSPI in 1991, and the 1991 publications committee, whose idea it was to create the series: Esther Powers (1991 NSPI president), Roger Addison (1992 NSPI president), William Coscarelli (1992 vice president of publications and president-elect), and Kathleen Whiteside (1993 NSPI president)—who led their boards of directors in providing emotional and financial support for the series from the beginning to the present; the topic editors and authors of the series, who through vision, intelligence, and perseverance transformed the idea of the series into the book you are now reading; Sarah Polster, editor of the management series at Jossey-Bass, who taught us what the business of publishing was all about, helped formulate the final look, feel, and chapter structure, negotiated the sometimes rough waters between our dreams about the series and what could actually be done, and coordinated the learning everyone at both NSPI and Jossey-Bass did about working together and producing a state-of-the-art series using state-of-the-art technology; Barbara Hill at Jossey-Bass, who coordinated all the deadlines, manuscripts, authors, reviewers, and many other things we're glad not to have to know about; James Jackson, manager of information technology training at Amoco Corporation, who saw the value of the series and my involvement in it and continually and generously supported my efforts.

Dedication

This series is dedicated to a forgotten leader in the HPT field and in NSPI: the 1963 "Man of the Year in Programming," whose ideas formed the early basis for HPT's processes and interventions; a visionary who challenged the status quo, always with logic, reason, and passion; a teacher, guide, and friend who pushed his students to exemplary performance, encouraged them also to challenge the status quo, assisted them in their journey, and then rewarded their successes lavishly; the series is dedicated to the late James D. Finn, with respect and thanks for all he gave to me personally as my mentor, to those (too numerous to mention) who knew and worked with him, and to the field and profession of Human Performance Technology.

Chicago, Illinois   Kenneth H. Silber
January 1994   Series editor

Designing the Work Environment for Optimum Performance: About This Group of Books

What is the purpose of these books?

- "Ever since I moved to this new office, I go home with a backache every night."
- "The only way I can get any work done around here is to hide in the cafeteria."
- "I suppose the new computer system would save us time—if anyone around here could figure out how to use it."

Have you ever heard statements like these in your workplace? Have you been known to make some of them yourself? Complaints about too much noise, too little light, uncomfortable chairs, cramped storage, or perplexing equipment may be a cue that the work environment is getting in the way of good performance.

What exactly is a "work environment"? It includes the resources that are available to perform the work, the design of the work, the tools in the environment, and how well the tools match human capabilities. Performance can suffer if any of these environmental factors are unavailable, inaccessible, or inadequate (Bullock, 1981; Rummler and Brache, 1990).

Improving the work environment has rich potential for improving human performance. This topic, which we explore in three books that discuss designing the work environment for optimum performance, is grounded in the philosophical belief that it is both easier and more effective to manipulate a problematic work environment than to change the people who must function in that environment. To put it simply, this approach says, *Don't fix the worker, fix the workplace.* The three books in this group tell you how to use the approach to create work environments that support rather than hinder performance.

How do these books fit in the series?

The books in this group are a subset of the series From Training to Performance in the Twenty-First Century. They focus on the input that a performer receives while doing work (see Figure P.4). They help readers discover whether the work environment, which is an essential component of this input, is adequate to support the desired performance. They then offer strategies for redesigning inadequate work environments.

Figure P.4. Work Environment as an Element of Input in the Human Performance System.

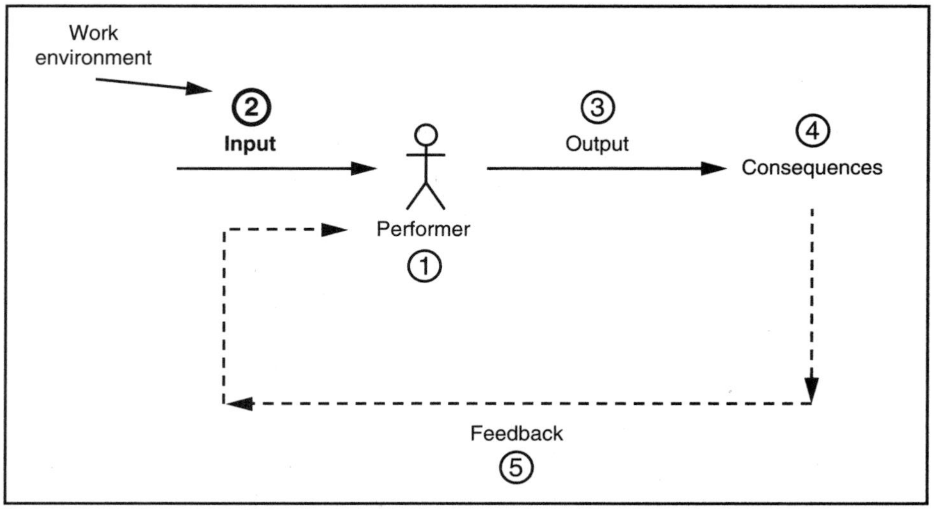

Source: Rummler and Brache, 1992, p.38

Creating the Ergonomically Sound Workplace, by Lee Ostrom, provides a basic understanding of the principles and methods of ergonomics. The procedures in the book will help you prevent worker injury by implementing such strategies as redesigning workstation layout, simplifying repetitive tasks, improving lifting tasks, and adjusting lighting.

Whereas Ostrom's book deals with the impact of the workplace on the body, *Creating Workplaces Where People Can Think,* by Phyl Smith and Lynn Kearny, is concerned with the impact of workplace design on the mind. The procedures in this book will help you identify attention-demanding features of the workplace that interfere with mental processing and redesign work areas to meet individual and group needs for privacy, stimulation, and communication.

Ostrom's and Smith and Kearny's books take a general view of work environment problems and solutions. *Making Computers People-Literate,* by Elaine Weiss, zeroes in on a specific tool that is increasingly present in work environments: the computer. The procedures in the book will help you improve the performance of computer users by conducting a targeted review of the computer system, identifying flaws in its user interface, and recommending redesigns to improve the interface.

Salt Lake City, Utah   Elaine Weiss
January 1994   Topic editor

Preface

Creating the Ergonomically Sound Workplace is a guide to the basic principles and methods of ergonomics as they apply to common workplace situations. Ergonomics has been defined by Grandjean (1990) as fitting the workplace to the person who works in it. After reading this book, you will be able to walk through a workplace, detect basic workplace design problems, and correct many of them yourself in order to prevent musculoskeletal injuries and the accompanying pain and disability among employees, improve employee performance, and reduce business costs associated with these injuries and illnesses.

The book focuses on the things in the workplace that you have control over and can successfully change, such as the adjustment of workstations, basic workplace layout, lighting, glare, and to a limited degree, task design. I urge you to seek further knowledge from other books and publications or the advice of an experienced ergonomist if you are challenged by more complex problems than this book covers.

Audience

Creating the Ergonomically Sound Workplace can be used by anyone in any organization. Individual workers can use it to learn what physical factors affect their own work. Managers at all levels can use it to help their employees work more comfortably and with fewer injuries, with the result that the organization retains skilled employees and maintains productivity levels.

Step-by-step procedures and worksheets and detailed illustrations make the book appropriate for both people who have no training in or experience with ergonomics and those who are familiar with ergonomic principles and are looking for a reliable set of tools for applying those principles.

Overview of the contents

Section One (Chapter One) contains an introduction to the basic principles of ergonomics. The simplified model of the workplace that I have developed features three elements: posture, activities, and environment. In this section, I explain the various areas of ergonomics as they apply to each workplace element and as they affect the employee's health and well-being.

Section Two (Chapters Two through Six) details procedures that can be used to improve workplace design. Chapter Two describes how to gather ergonomic data from or about individuals, how to interview employees and their managers, and how to review the rate of illness and injury in an area. Chapter Three presents procedures that you can apply to improve employee posture by adjusting workstations to fit individual employees. Chapter Four covers procedures for improving the activities employees perform so that the activities will not cause illness or injury.

The procedures in Chapter Five are designed to help you improve the workplace environment, especially the lighting. Suggestions for reducing glare from video display terminals are also included. Chapter Six describes a procedure for conducting follow-ups to ergonomic assessments, to ensure that ergonomic adjustments are working as you intended and to alter them if necessary.

Section Three (Chapter Seven) presents a case study that shows how the procedures are applied in a typical workplace.

Section Four contains six resources. Resource A is a worksheet (OSHA Form 200) used to review illness and injury statistics. Resources B, C, D, and E contain worksheet forms that you can photocopy to use when you apply the procedures described in Section Two. Resource B consists of worksheets to use in procedures for interviewing employees and managers. Resource C is a worksheet for organizing an ergonomic assessment of a workplace. Resource D contains worksheets for assessing sitting and standing workstations with and without video display terminals, as well as workstation layout and lighting and tasks involving lifting and repetitive motion. The worksheets in Resource E will help you select chairs and workstations that fit, or can be adjusted to fit, individual employees. Resource F is a comprehensive glossary of the special terms used in this book.

I hope that you will use the book as a resource to continually improve working conditions in your workplace. Musculoskeletal injuries and illnesses are painful and can be disabling and expensive to treat. Anything that can be done to reduce the incidence of these conditions helps all of us to enjoy better, healthier workplaces and, indeed, happier lives.

Acknowledgments

I wish to acknowledge many individuals for their guidance and support in this project. First, I would like to thank the topic and series editors, Elaine Weiss and Kenneth Silber, for their comments and support. I wish to thank William Nelson and Harold Blackman, my boss and my boss's boss, for their support and understanding. Thanks go also to Cheryl Wilhelmsen and Henry Romero for their general support. And especially, I would like to express my gratitude to James L. Smith for his comments on the manuscript and his guidance during my doctoral training.

Finally, I wish to thank my wife, Mary Beth, my daughter, Laura, and my son, John (who heard me say, "I need to go work on the book," far too many times), for their loving patience and understanding.

Idaho Falls, Idaho   Lee T. Ostrom
January 1994

The Author

Lee T. Ostrom is senior scientist with EG&G Idaho, at the Idaho National Engineering Laboratory. He received a B.S. degree (1979) in bacteriology from the University of Idaho. He received an M.S. degree (1980) in Interdisciplinary studies with an emphasis on occupational safety and health from Texas Tech University. He received a Ph.D. degree (1988) in industrial engineering, specializing in ergonomics, also from Texas Tech University. Ostrom's research interests are in the areas of ergonomics and human error, and he is currently involved in researching the causes of accidents in nuclear medicine. He has written articles on manual materials handling, workplace design, physical training, human reliability analysis, and organizational factors. Ostrom has been designated a Certified Professional Ergonomist by the Board of Certification in Professional Ergonomics. He is a member of the Human Factors Society, the American Institute of Aeronautics and Astronautics, and the Institute of Industrial Engineers. He has also received the Certified Safety Professional designation from the Board of Certified Safety Professionals. He lives in Idaho with his wife and two children.

CREATING THE ERGONOMICALLY SOUND WORKPLACE

HOW THE PHYSICAL WORK ENVIRONMENT AFFECTS PERFORMANCE

Overview

What is this section about?

This section defines ergonomics, describes the injuries and illnesses related to workplace ergonomics, and defines typical injuries and illnesses. Basic principles of ergonomics that are important to an understanding of good and bad workplace posture, activities, and environment are discussed, along with measurable outcomes of ergonomically sound practices.

How is this section organized?

CHAPTER 1

What are the Benefits of Ergonomic Workspace Design?

Introduction

What is ergonomics?

The word *ergonomics* is derived from two Greek words: *ergon,* which means "work," and *nomos,* which means "laws." Therefore, ergonomics, in its most general sense, means the "laws of work." Etienne Grandjean (1990) has defined ergonomics more specifically as fitting the task to the person. How you and your employees can achieve a fit to your tasks is the subject of this book. Terms used interchangeably with ergonomics are *human factors* and *human engineering.* When I suggest that certain problems require the expertise of an *ergonomist,* I am referring to a person who specializes in matching the demands of jobs to the capabilities and limitations of the people who perform the jobs.

Standardized production and repetitive motion

For almost two centuries, industry in the United States has been striving to standardize its production methods. In doing so, it has forced employees to adapt to the workplace, rather than adapting the workplace to the employees' capabilities and limitations. However, researchers have found that workers who perform tasks that are not designed to fit the workers' capabilities and limitations and who work at workstations that are not adjusted to them have a higher potential for developing musculoskeletal injuries than workers who have ergonomically designed tasks and workstations.

Companies standardized their production lines following the concepts of Eli Whitney and Frederick Taylor, both of whom worked primarily in the nineteenth century. Before 1800, most manufactured goods made in the United States were one-of-a-kind items produced by family-run shops or small community industries. Craftsmen built or forged their own tools and arranged their own work areas. Therefore, their tools and workplaces were designed to fit them.

The concept of interchangeable parts, introduced by Eli Whitney around 1800, changed this pattern of production (Current, Williams, and Freidel, 1975). Whitney developed his concept when the U.S. military wanted muskets that were repairable in the field. At that time, each musket was handmade and therefore unique. Parts were not interchangeable. If a musket broke, the soldier had to find a new weapon or a gunsmith to repair the broken one. Also, the military needed 10,000 muskets for an undeclared war with France, but there were not enough gunsmiths in the country to make that many guns. Whitney set up a factory to make standardized parts for muskets and then hired workers to assemble the parts into the final product.

The introduction of standardized parts into manufacturing was one of two major steps that brought about an industrial culture in which a "job" was made up of very few tasks.

Frederick Taylor is credited with implementing the second major step in the process of industrial standardization: creating standardized tasks (Barnes, 1980). In the late 1800s and early 1900s, Taylor timed workers performing tasks and found that manufacturing seemed most efficient if workers repeatedly performed the same limited set of motions. After Taylor's discoveries, workers who once might have taken a design from raw materials to finished product now performed only a very few repetitive tasks and, along with the tasks, a very few repetitive motions. Individualism was gone; jobs and products had become standardized.

Thus, from the turn of the twentieth century till the early 1980s, workers in manufacturing workplaces typically performed repetitive tasks. Once tasks were standardized, a worker might be assigned a task comprising only a few hand and arm motions, and the worker would perform that task thousands of times per day, day in and day out. Not only were the tasks standardized, the workplaces, too, were standardized. The shapes of chairs, heights of desks and workbenches, weights of loads, and sizes of tools were all set by certain standards. Employers also provided only standard fifteen-minute rest breaks at standard times. This standardization of tasks and workplaces has taken its toll on the U.S. workforce as workers, who come in different shapes and with different abilities, have had to adapt to standardized workplaces. And the physical results of this method of standardization have been musculoskeletal injuries and illnesses.

Today, the concept of job enrichment has started to reverse this trend toward standardized tasks. Companies that have adopted the job enrichment concept are broadening the scope of jobs because they have found that workers who do a variety of tasks are more interested in the jobs and perform them better. The concept of job enrichment has not been universally adopted, however. Most jobs still require workers to perform a limited number of tasks. Also, as more and more tasks are computerized, workers are spending more time on personal computers. So even when workers are asked to do a larger variety of tasks, they may still be doing them at one workstation, a computer workstation.

Injuries Caused by Workplace Design

What are musculoskeletal injuries and illnesses?

Injuries that are caused by workplace design have been called a variety of names including *cumulative trauma disorders, repetitive motion syndromes,* and *musculoskeletal injuries.* I use the terms musculoskeletal injuries and cumulative trauma disorders (CTDs), which are considered illnesses. Most of these injuries and illnesses involve the soft tissues of the body, primarily muscles, ligaments, and tendons. The problems usually result from repeated microtraumas of these soft tissues. However, they can also be caused by a single trauma, for example, lifting a heavy object incorrectly. Back strains and sprains are the most common musculoskeletal injuries (National Safety Council, 1990).

Kroemer (1992) explains what actually occurs in soft tissues as a result of repetitive trauma. Strains occur when muscles are overstretched, resulting in muscle aching and swelling.

Tendons do not stretch. When they are injured, they can become rough or even fray. As a result, they do not glide past other tissue as easily as they should and excessive amounts of synovial fluid are produced. In small amounts, synovial fluid helps tendons slide through tendon sheaths; in excess amounts, it causes tendon sheaths to swell and become inflammed.

Nerves that are injured by repeated or sustained pressure have reduced nerve conduction. This can cause numbness, tingling, or pain in the affected body part. Carpal tunnel syndrome, for instance, is a CTD resulting from the compression of the median nerve in the wrist.

Finally, problems can occur when blood vessels are compressed, reducing blood flow and cutting off nutrients to the tissue downstream. Table 1.1 lists the common cumulative trauma disorders and the part of the body affected.

Diseases with similar symptoms

It is important to be aware that disease can also cause some of these conditions and symptoms. For instance, any disease that causes swelling of the wrists (Lyme's Disease, for example) can also cause carpal tunnel syndrome. Therefore, when an employee complains of a physical problem, he or she needs to see a physician in order to rule out certain diseases before modifications are made to the workplace.

Table 1.1. Common Cumulative Trauma Disorders.

Disorder	Description
Carpal tunnel syndrome (CTS)	A compression of the median nerve in the carpal tunnel (*carpal* means relating to the wrist) by tendons that also pass through the carpal tunnel. CTS is linked to performing highly repetitive tasks, like typing or cutting meat, with the wrist deviated.
Epicondylitis (tennis elbow)	An irritation of the tendons attached to the epicondyle (a knob of bone at the elbow end of the humerus, the upper arm bone). This condition is often the result of impacting or jerky throwing motions or repeated rotation of the forearm. Tasks like wrapping wire are linked to this condition.
Neck tension	An irritation of a group of muscles related to the neck: the levator scapulae (literally, shoulder blade lifter) and trapezius (a flat triangular upper-back muscle). Neck tension commonly occurs after repeated or sustained overhead work. It is also linked to tasks like typing, proofreading, assembling small parts, and using a microscope.
Tendinitis	An inflammation of a tendon, the tissue that connects muscles to bones. Often associated with repeated tensioning of the tendon, tendinitis is linked to tasks requiring numerous repetitious motions, like meat-cutting and assembly work.
Trigger finger	A special case of tendinitis in which a tendon becomes nearly locked and its forced movement is not smooth. Trigger finger is most common in the fingers and the thumbs.
Tenosynovitis	A disorder that occurs when a tendon is repeatedly tensed, causing an excess release of synovial fluid from the synovial sheath through which the tendon passes.

Table 1.1. (Continued)

Disorder	Description
de Quervain's syndrome	A special case of tenosynovitis that occurs in the abductor and extensor tendons of the thumb at the point where they share a common sheath. The syndrome is linked with tasks that require numerous thumb motions, such as operating a track ball or a screwgun.
Thoracic outlet syndrome (TOS)	A compression of the nerves and blood vessels between the clavicle (collarbone) and first and second ribs at the brachial plexus (a nerve network for the shoulder, arm, and chest). TOS is linked with such tasks as obtaining numerous files from a tall cabinet.

Source. Adapted from Kroemer, 1992, pp. 596-604.

Costs of musculoskeletal injuries and illnesses

Back injuries are one class of musculoskeletal injury. In 1990, back injuries alone accounted for 22 percent of all disabling occupational injuries and 32 percent of all workers' compensation costs in the United States (National Safety Council, 1990). The 22 percent figure equates to 380,000 injuries. Andersson (1981), Snook (1982), and Klein, Roger, Jensen, and Sanderson (1984) have linked back injuries with workplace and task design.

Cumulative trauma disorders (CTDs) are another class of musculoskeletal injury. CTDs include carpal tunnel syndrome, tendinitis, and trigger finger (see Table 1.1). A recent study by Brogmus and Marko (1992) of Liberty Mutual Insurance Group shows the magnitude of the CTD problem in this country. CTDs made up 2 percent of all cases Liberty Mutual paid in 1991 and represented 3.5 percent of all Liberty Mutual's costs. The average cost of a CTD claim to the insurance company was $10,000, although, of course, individual cases varied considerably: those that required surgery and extensive physical therapy would have cost more and those that required very little intervention—for example, a slight workplace modification—would have cost less.

Medical costs are not the only expense connected with workplace injuries. There are hidden costs as well: the cost to train a new employee if one becomes disabled, the cost to employee morale, and the loss of the use of those funds spent on medical bills, funds that otherwise could be used for other business purposes. Most important is the cost to the employee in terms of lost income, pain, and the possibility that he or she will never regain full function of the affected body part.

Researchers including Ayoub and Mital (1989), Chaffin and Andersson (1984), Grandjean (1990), Putz-Anderson (1988), and as a host of others have found that ergonomic interventions, for instance, correctly adjusting a desk to an individual, can reduce the incidence of musculoskeletal injuries. In numerous cases, the workplace intervention costs less than the medical and other costs associated with a musculoskeletal injury. For example, the average cost of an average case of carpal tunnel syndrome is $10,000, but the cost of properly adjusting a desk is minimal in comparison. An intervention that may take fifteen minutes can save thousands of dollars as well as pain, discomfort, and decrement in employee morale.

The Three Key Principles of Ergonomics

The three key principles of ergonomics are

- Fit the task and workplace to the individual
- Design the workplace for individuals with a range of body sizes
- Design the workplace for individuals at the extremes of the body-size range

Fit the task and workplace to the individual

A workplace should be designed to accommodate the individual's physical needs rather than to force the individual to fit the workplace (Grandjean, 1990; Ayoub and Mital, 1989). For instance, if an engineer designs a task that requires a person to lift 100-pound weights every ten seconds, there is no amount of training, motivation, or incentive that will give most people the ability to perform this task. It is beyond most individuals' physical work capacity. Even if an employee tried to perform this task, he or she would probably become fatigued and/or injured very quickly.

This is an obvious example of poor design, but many poor designs are not so immediately apparent unless we accustom ourselves to looking for the repetitive motions and poor posture that work may require of employees.

Thus, we must carefully consider people's working capacities when we design tasks and workstations. If only one person will be performing the task, the task needs to be tailored to that individual to the greatest extent possible. If numerous employees will be using the same workplace or workstation, then the remaining two principles of ergonomics need to be applied.

Design for a range of body sizes

Typically, a workplace or product must be designed to accommodate a wide range of individuals. If a six-foot-tall engineer designs a chair to fit only himself or herself, it probably will not fit an individual who is only five feet tall. Over time, the five-foot-tall individual may develop an musculo-skeletal injury for using such a chair. If the chair is used at a computer workstation and the user's feet don't touch the floor, the circulation in the user's lower legs would be cut off, and they would keep falling asleep.

Therefore, when designing workplaces, adjustments need to be allowed for so that a wide range of individuals can use the product safely. The size of the range is determined by the population to be served.

All we have to do is walk down a street in a busy city or go to a public event to see the vast range of people's sizes and shapes. This range of sizes will change, however, depending on the *population* we must accommodate in the workplace. For example, the range of sizes and shapes is huge if we consider all the people in the world as our population. The range of sizes narrows somewhat if we restrict our population to all the people in the United States. In particular, the range of the most common sizes and shapes changes. The range is further restricted if our population includes only drivers between the ages of sixteen and sixty-five. The range of sizes within a large corporation may be quite large, but within one work unit, the population may be more restricted. Therefore, before we design a workplace, we need to define the population we are trying to accommodate.

Everyone within a designated population will belong to a particular *percentile* of that population. Webster's Encyclopedic Dictionary of the English Language defines percentile as "any of the points dividing a range of data into 100 equal intervals and indicating the percentage of a distribution falling below it." For example, if we measured the heights, or statures, of a population consisting of ten adult workers, the heights might range from 58 inches to 76 inches. Each individual's height percentile would depend on where in the range he or she fell. If the individual heights of the ten workers are 50, 60, 63, 65, 66, 68, 69, 70, 71, and 76 inches, the worker who is 63 inches tall is in the 30th percentile because 30 percent of the workforce is equal to or less than that height. The worker who is 70 inches tall is in the 80th percentile because 80 percent of the workforce is equal to or less than that height. Similarly, the 58-inch-tall worker is in the 10th percentile and the 76-inch-tall worker is in the 100th percentile.

The range of sizes a design usually needs to cover is the 5th to the 95th percentile. This will cover 90 percent of the population to be served, thus ensuring that most individuals can use the product or workplace without problem. People at the extremes of the population curve, the upper or lower 5 percent, can be significantly different in body dimensions from the rest of the population. They will require products and workplaces that are designed specifically for them.

The inclusion of adjustments in designs for workplaces and tools is not always possible, and therefore, workplace designers may also need products of varying sizes to fit the workplace population. Tool handles are a good example. A hammer handle that fits a 95th percentile male will be too large for a 5th percentile female. So employers and managers may need to have a range of tools and workplace furniture available for their employees' use.

No one would expect a 95th percentile male to wear the clothes designed for a 5th percentile female. Even if the style were unisex, the clothes simply wouldn't fit. Businesses are now learning that workplaces aren't that different from clothes in this regard and that it is only logical to have products and workplaces that are designed to accommodate those who will be using them.

Design for the extremes of a range

Workplaces or products should be chosen or designed so that the person with the most extreme dimensions in the 5th to 95th percentile range can be accommodated. For example, if a lifting task is designed to accommodate only a 95th percentile male's lifting capacity, there is no way a 5th percentile female can perform the task. Therefore, the lifting task needs to be designed so that the person with the lowest lifting capacity in the particular population is accommodated. If a control panel is designed so that only a 95th percentile male can reach the knobs, then a 5th percentile female cannot possibly reach them. If a workstation's thigh clearance is designed for a 5th percentile female, the station then will be too small for a 95th percentile male. Thus, it is important for those designing or selecting tools, tasks, and workplaces to determine the population and the percentiles who will use different products, and to meet that population's specific needs.

Training is not a substitute for sound design

Training individuals to overcome workplace and task design problems does not work because people cannot go beyond their physical limits. For example:

- An employee cannot be trained to reach something that is beyond his or her normal reach.

- An employee cannot be trained to lift a container that weighs more than his or her lifting capacity.

- An employee cannot be trained to attain a posture that puts a great deal of force on his or her back.

Even when employees can adapt to a poorly designed workplace for a time, the ultimate result is bad for the individual and for the larger society. Sweatshops, for example, set up business in areas where there is an excess of labor. It does not matter to the sweatshops if the employees in these poorly designed workplaces stay healthy because there is always another body to take the place of a disabled employee. However, there is an enormous cost to the individual employee and to the society that must now support that person.

Employees should be trained about the causes of musculoskeletal injuries, however, so they can identify work habits and workplace designs that lead to injuries. By knowing, for instance, that a certain wrist posture can cause carpal tunnel syndrome an employee will know to avoid that wrist posture. Employees also should be trained about taking breaks to overcome the fatigue brought on by work. Procedure 4.2 in Section Two outlines what should be included in a training program concerning the causes of CTDs and procedure 4.4 outlines what should be included in a training program concerning lifting and back injuries. Physical fitness training will also help the employee to stay healthy, but training of any sort is no substitute for proper workplace design.

Areas of the workplace that require design

Section Two of this book presents procedures to determine if there are mismatches between employees and their workstations and how to correct such mismatches. The ergonomic criteria used in these procedures are based on ergonomic theories derived from scientific studies of human capacities and from historical data on the causes of musculoskeletal injuries and illnesses. These ergonomic theories relate to three aspects of a workplace or task:

- The posture required by the workplace (see page 13)
- The activities associated with the workplace (see page 22)
- The environment of the workplace (see page 26)

Figure 1.1. Effect of Posture on the Forces Acting on the Back.

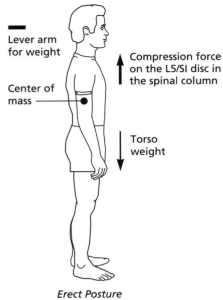

Lever arm for weight

Center of mass

Compression force on the L5/SI disc in the spinal column

Torso weight

Erect Posture
Desirable

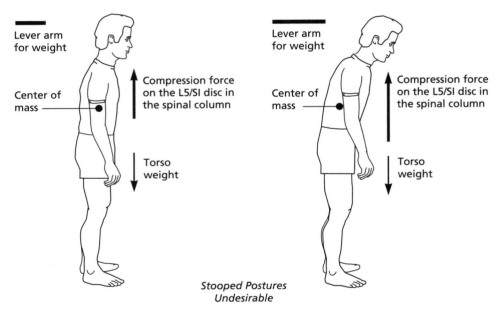

Lever arm for weight

Center of mass

Compression force on the L5/SI disc in the spinal column

Torso weight

Lever arm for weight

Center of mass

Compression force on the L5/SI disc in the spinal column

Torso weight

Stooped Postures
Undesirable

Note: The L5/S1 disc is the 5th Lumbar/1st sacral vertibral disc and is considered in most biomechanical models to be the fulcrum for the human body.

Theories of Ergonomics Related to Posture

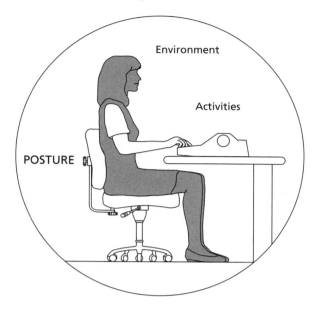

In general there are four primary postures employees are required to attain to perform work: sitting, standing, kneeling, and lying down. This book discusses only the most common workplace postures: standing and sitting.

There are two areas of ergonomic research that deal with posture: anthropometry and biomechanics. Anthropometry is an empirical science concerned with people's physical measurements. Anthropometric data is used to fit the workplace and the task to the person. Occupational biomechanics deals with the stresses on body parts that result from the design of tasks and workplaces. The ergonomist's goal is to design the workplace and task to meet the anthropometric requirements of the employee and thus help the employee attain a good posture. The result of a good posture is the minimization of biomechanical stresses on the body (Chaffin and Andersson, 1984). Of course, what is good for one person may be uncomfortable to another. So there is no one good posture. Instead, the ultimate judge of what is good is the employee.

What is good posture? A large amount of research has been conducted to determine what constitutes a good posture, one that minimizes the biomechanical stresses on the body. This research has shown that good sitting and standing postures are like those shown in Figures 1.1 and 1.2. As you can see, in a good standing posture, the person's back is straight, and the head is in line with the shoulder and hip joint. In a good sitting posture, the knees are bent at a ninety-degree angle. The biomechanical stresses on the back are minimized in this posture. In particular, the compression forces on the vertebral discs of the back are low when the person is sitting in a good posture and even lower when the person is in a good standing posture.

We all know that weight acts only in one direction—down, toward the center of the earth—because weight is the result of gravity. The human body maneuvers weight by acting somewhat like a system of levers. The bones make up the levers. The muscles move the bones. The connective tissues (like ligaments) hold the bones and muscles together. Other structures, such as tendon sheaths, help the connective tissues and muscles to move smoothly. The body, however, has very poor mechanical advantage.

Figure 1.2. How Workplace Arrangement Affects Posture.

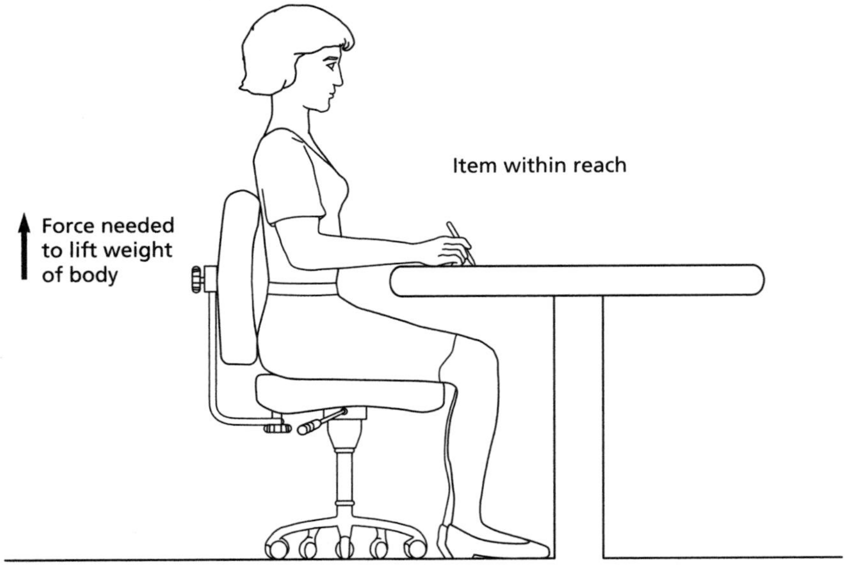

Force needed to lift weight of body

Item within reach

Desirable Posture

Force needed to lift weight of body

Employee has to lean forward to grab item

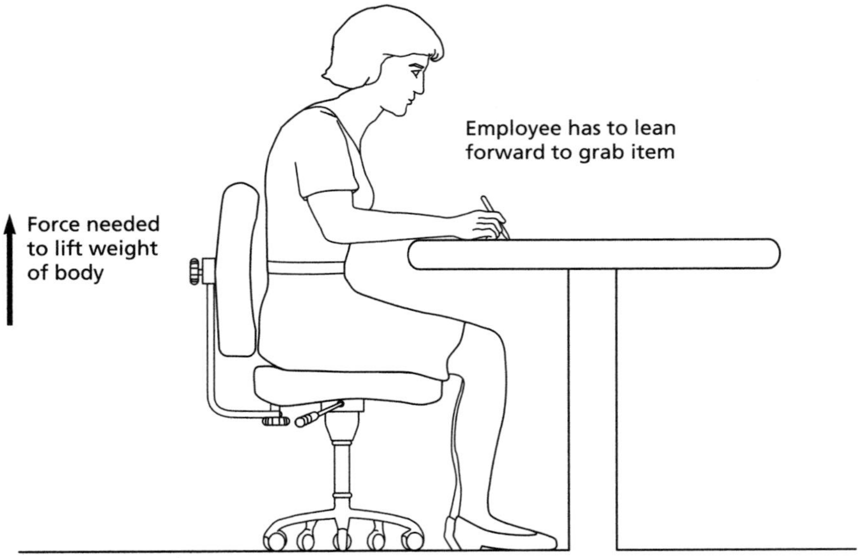

Undesirable Posture

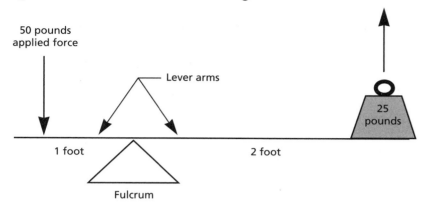

Figure 1.3. Poor Mechanical Advantage.

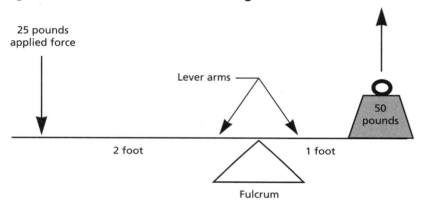

Figure 1.4. Good Mechanical Advantage.

The concept of mechanical advantage is illustrated in Figures 1.3 and 1.4. In Figure 1.3, a lever system with poor mechanical advantage, the lever arm for the fifty pounds of applied force is shorter than the lever arm for the twenty-five pound weight to which it is applied. The mechanical advantage in this illustration is only one half, that is, it takes twice as much applied force as the weight weighs to lift the weight. In Figure 1.4, a lever system with good mechanical advantage, the lever arm for the applied force is twice the length of the lever arm for the weight. Thus, the mechanical advantage is two. The body's lever systems are like the one in Figure 1.3, although the exact degree of mechanical advantage varies for each lever.

The body has poor mechanical advantage because the levers it possesses to apply force are usually short in relation to the lever arm of the weight to be moved. One weight the body must cope with all the time is its own weight. Figure 1.1 shows how posture affects the lever system in the back. Poor posture lengthens the lever arm for the weight of the torso, and that lengthening increases the relative amount of force needed to overcome gravity as it acts on the body.

The more force a person needs to overcome gravity the more quickly he or she becomes fatigued. Fatigue can lead to musculoskeletal injury. So, workplaces and tasks need to be designed so that people can work in postures that decrease rather than increase the stresses the work places on their bodies. Lever arms for lifting weight should be as short as possible in relation to the lever arms for applying force.

The arrangement of the workplace also can affect posture. Figure 1.2 illustrates how the employee can attain a good posture when he or she is close to the work and items are placed within his or her reach. However, the forces on the back are increased when the employee has to lean forward to reach for something beyond his or her normal reach. The design of the workplace should also allow tasks to be performed with arms close to the body and below the shoulder level. Biomechanical forces are always increased the farther the employee has to reach.

Should employees sit in the same posture all day? The answer to this question is no. Although a good posture minimizes the forces on the back, the posture should not be rigid, and the employee should have the ability to shift posture frequently during the day. The reason for this is that the muscles act as a pump to help move the blood, which carries oxygen and nutrients to tissue (Grandjean, 1990). When an employee sits in any posture for too long, blood flow may be restricted, with the result that tissues may become weakened and more susceptible to injury. This is true for any part of the body, so the workplace should allow the employee to attain a full range of motion so he or she can stretch and improve the circulation of the blood. Employees should also have their desks or workstations arranged so that they can achieve the good posture that is most comfortable to them.

Upper extremity posture. Postures of body parts other than the spine also affect the potential for developing a musculoskeletal injury or illness. For instance, when the wrist is deviated, held in other than a neutral posture, the potential for developing carpal tunnel syndrome increases. Figure 1.5 shows two views of the neutral wrist posture and the four ways the wrist can be deviated. The tendons that cause the fingers to curl run through the carpal tunnel of the wrist. The median nerve and some of the blood vessels of the hand also run through the carpal tunnel. When the fingers are repeatedly flexed, the tendons can swell (Putz-Anderson, 1988). This swelling puts pressure on the median nerve, thus reducing nerve conduction, and over time, this pressure on the nerve can cause permanent disability. This fact does not mean that employees should never adopt a bad wrist or body posture, but it does make clear that the amount of time an employee spends in a bad posture should be minimized.

Figure 1.5. Wrist Postures.

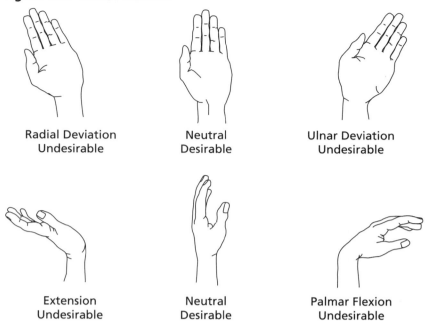

Radial Deviation
Undesirable

Neutral
Desirable

Ulnar Deviation
Undesirable

Extension
Undesirable

Neutral
Desirable

Palmar Flexion
Undesirable

Factors affecting posture

The factors in the workplace that can affect an employee's posture are

• Chair design
• Anthropometry
• Obstacles

Chair design. A properly designed chair is one of the most important pieces of equipment in a workplace that requires sitting (Grandjean, 1987) because chair design has a major impact on an employee's sitting posture. A chair does not have to be expensive or have all the optional bells and whistles to be effective. What it does need to do is fit the employee. Once again, the employee should not be expected to adopt a bad posture in order to fit the chair he or she has been given. Like all ergonomic equipment, chairs are individual, and what works for one employee may not work for another. Employees should have the opportunity to try out the chairs they will be using before the company purchases them. Employees may be sitting in these chairs for eight hours or more every day, and they should like the way the chairs feel. Also, it is imperative that employees be shown how to adjust their chairs. The brochure that comes with a chair usually contains information about how to adjust the chair.

**Figure 1.6. Anthropometric Data for Sitting Postures.
(In Inches.)**

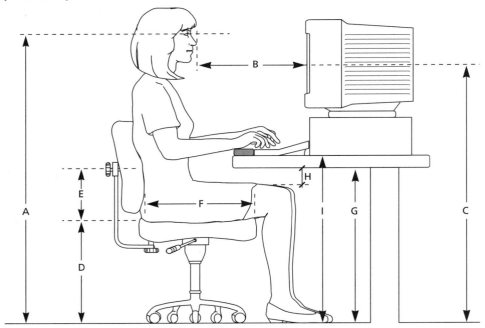

A. Distance of eyes from floor
B. Distance of eyes from VDT screen
C. Distance of center of VDT screen from floor
D. Distance of top of seat pan, compressed, from floor
E. Distance of center of lumbar support from top of compressed seat pan
F. Distance of lumbar support from front of seat pan
G. Distance of underside of work surface from floor
H. Vertical and horizontal knee clearance under work surface
I. Distance of keyboard from floor (approximates elbow height)

Anthropometry. The posture an employee adopts in a workplace that has not been adjusted depends partly on his or her body dimensions. In Section Two of this book you will be shown how to adjust the workplace to the individual so that he or she can attain good posture. Anthropometric data collected from various populations and contained in data bases such as those in *Humanscale* (Diffrient, Tilley, and Harmon, 1991), *Bodyspace: Anthropometry, Ergonomics, and Design* (Pheasant, 1986), and the *Human Engineering Guide to Equipment Design* (Van Cott and Kinkade, 1972) can be used to set up a workstation to fit someone in a certain percentile of the population.

Anthropometric researchers have also produced regression equations that are easy to use to approximate a person's various body dimensions if the measurement of another dimension is known. For instance, height is used as an input in several of these equations to estimate average heights of eyes and knees and, therefore, average heights of work surfaces and video display terminals (VDTs). The most important anthropometric dimensions for sitting postures in offices are shown in Figure 1.6 and for standing postures in Figure 1.7. The regression equations in Table 1.2 and Table 1.3 use an individual's known height, or stature, to generate approximate figures for the additional anthropometric data needed in Figures 1.6 and 1.7.

Figure 1.7. Anthropometric Data for Standing Postures.

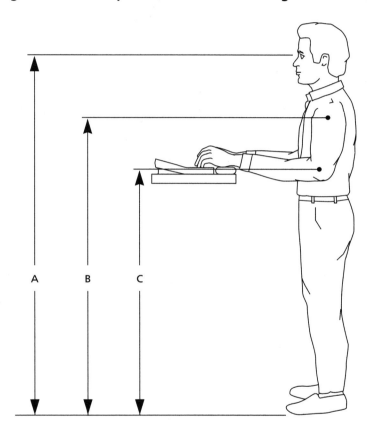

A. Distance of eyes from floor

B. Distance of shoulder joint from floor

C. Distance of elbow joint from floor

Table 1.2: Equations for Anthropometric Data for Sitting Postures.

A = (0.726 × STATURE) − 2.167
B = (0.412 × STATURE) − 0.240
C = (0.605 × STATURE) − 3.886
D = (0.271 × STATURE) − 1.706
E = (0.148 × STATURE) − 3.732
F = (0.081 × STATURE) + 10.017
G = (0.295 × STATURE) + 4.213
H = (0.331 × STATURE) − 5.310
I = (0.331 × STATURE) + 3.142

Source. Romero, Ostrom, and Wilhelmsen, 1993.

Table 1.3: Equations for Anthropometric Data for Standing Postures.

A = 0.936 × STATURE
B = 0.818 × STATURE
C = 0.63 × STATURE

Source. Adapted from Roebuck, Kroemer, and Thomson, 1975.

For example, equation I in Table 1.2 determines an average height for a keyboard for employees of a known height. To use the equation, determine the employee's height, for example, 70 inches. Enter this figure into the equation: I = (0.331 × 70) + 3.142 = 26.3 inches. Thus, the *average* height of a keyboard for a 70-inch-tall employee is 26.3 inches. Calculating the average anthropometric data for a workplace population will suggest the ranges within which workplaces must be adjustable. Remember, however, that the most important criterion is the posture of the employee in relation to the workstation and not a workstation set up to some standard.

Be aware of the "myth of the average man." No one is average. Everyone varies in some or most body measurements from what he or she should measure according to his or her percentile height. For example, individuals in the same height percentile may have longer or shorter reach distances than predicted. Van Cott and Kinkade (1972) state that the key to successful workplace design is adjustability. If a workplace is designed for adjustability, it will accommodate a wider range of individuals. The best way to use anthropometric data is as a starting point for workplace design. From this point, the workstation can be adjusted to the individual. Anthropometric data tells designers the range of body sizes that should be accommodated by a particular design; it does not predict a specific individual's every measurement.

Obstacles and housekeeping. Obstacles in the workplace can hinder a person from attaining a good posture. For example, clutter under a desk can prevent a person from getting close to his or her work. The location of file cabinets, desks, and other pieces of office equipment can effectively constrain an employee to adopt an undesirable posture. Slippery floors also contribute to the workplace's potential for musculoskeletal injuries (Leamon, 1993).

Guidelines

General guidelines to improve an employee's posture include the following:

- Adjust the workstation to fit the individual (see Chapter Three).
- Adjust the workstation so the employee can perform the task without deviating his or her wrists (see Chapters Three and Four).
- Place commonly used items within the easy reach (see Chapter Four). (This step also improves workplace activities.)
- Allow the employee the ability to shift postures easily.

Theories of Ergonomics Related to Activities

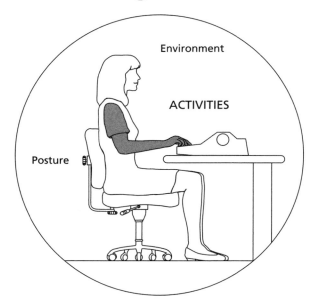

Numerous tasks are performed in workplaces. Even in offices, tasks can range from light assembly using hand tools, to paperwork and computer assignments, to instruction of others. These tasks can require lifting; use of the arms, hands, and shoulders; and/or a large amount of walking. Workplace activities can be described in terms of

- Repetition, or the number of times the task or a particular motion is performed
- Force needed to perform the task
- Amount of rest time provided

The areas of ergonomics that will be discussed in relation to activities are biomechanics, work physiology, psychophysics, and epidemiology.

Biomechanical forces

The key point about the biomechanics of activities that must be kept in mind is that, as the pace of an activity is increased, the forces acting on the body are increased because of the increase in the velocity and acceleration of the body parts used for performing the required motions. A task that is not very biomechanically stressful at a slow pace might be very stressful at fast pace. Therefore more rest time must be provided for faster-paced activities and/or the task must be redesigned to reduce the weight of the material handled or the force required to perform the activity.

Work physiology

Physiology is the science concerned with the normal function of living organs. Work in this context is defined as the amount of energy that is required to move a body part from one position to another. Therefore, work physiology is concerned with the living organs and systems that supply energy to move the body, or parts of the body (Astrand and Rodahl, 1986).

The systems that are of primary importance to work physiology are the respiratory system, circulatory system, central nervous system, and the muscles. (For a more thorough discussion of human physiology, the reader should refer to a physiology textbook such as Guyton, 1984.)

Physical work capacity (PWC) is one of the most important measurements in work physiology. Also called maximal aerobic power or maximum oxygen uptake (Rodahl, 1989; Astrand and Rodahl, 1986; McArdle, Katch, and Katch, 1986), PWC is the highest oxygen uptake an individual can attain during physical work while breathing air at sea level. PWC is a genetic attribute and training results in only a modest increase (Astrand and Rodahl, 1986; McArdle, Katch, and Katch, 1986).

There is a direct relationship between heart rate and oxygen uptake—as the heart beats faster, the body consumes more oxygen and thus more energy. The harder the task, the more rest the body needs to overcome fatigue caused by the physiological workload. PWC, the maximum uptake, occurs at a person's maximum heart rate, which is approximately 220 minus the person's age. The average PWC for males is approximately 3 liters of oxygen per minute (Astrand and Rodahl, 1986). For females, the average is approximately 2.5 liters per minute. The body utilizes five food calories for every liter of oxygen consumed.

Many studies have been conducted to determine at what percentage of PWC workers can perform for long periods of time. (Most of these studies focused on lifting activities.) The limit that has been suggested is approximately 33 percent of PWC (Garg and Ayoub, 1980). However, Mital (1983) also studied a limit based on 28 percent of PWC. At 33 percent of PWC, the average person's heart is beating at about 100 beats per minute, about the rate that walking at a normal pace would produce. At this pace, it appears workers can work all day without excessive fatigue. Therefore, when activities are designed or analyzed, consider the heart rate and the work pace. If the employee is working with a heart rate greater than 100 beats per minute, he or she probably needs longer and more frequent rest breaks. Fatigued employees have a high potential for musculoskeletal injuries or illnesses.

Even office workers can, at times, perform tasks that will cause their hearts to beat faster than 100 beats per minute (and not just at office parties). Moving boxes of files is one such task. In these instances, provide adequate time for the employee to recover from the task before starting a new task. Also, if the weight of the container to be moved or the force needed to perform a task is high, then reduce the frequency of the task. If the frequency cannot be reduced, then reduce the weight of the container or the force required.

| Psychophysics | Both biomechanics and work physiology deal with objectively defined limits of the body's capacity. Psychophysics deals with *perceived* limits to capacity. In biomechanics for example, a person's limits for lifting are based on the pressure at which vertebral discs will rupture. In work physiology, the limits are based on a person's PWC. But in psychophysics, the limits are based on what a person perceives his or her physical work limits to be. |

Psychophysics has been applied in many areas of the workplace. For example, Houghton and Yagloglou (1923) developed an effective temperature scale (see NIOSH, 1973, p. 420), and Stevens (1960) developed scales of perceived brightness. Foreman, Baxter, and Troup (1984) applied acceptability scaling to vertical isometric force applications at knee and waist level. Subjects were asked whether they felt they could hold a particular weight for two minutes, then asked to adjust a box to a weight they could actually hold for that time. The experiment proved to be repeatable. Psychophysics has been used by many researchers to determine people's capability to manually handle materials, including their lifting capacity (Ayoub and others, 1978; Karwowski, 1982; Jiang, 1984; Mital, 1980; Ostrom, 1988; and others), pushing and pulling capacity (Snook, 1978), ability to hold objects in unusual postures (Ayoub and others, 1988), and a variety of other tasks.

There are numerous instances in which psychophysical perceptions affect the performance of an activity in an office setting—for example, lifting boxes, typing, or performing light assembly tasks such as putting documents together. One finding of psychophysics is that employees who are provided with control of one variable associated with a task—for instance, the rate at which they assemble binders—will perform the task with a reduced potential for injury. Allowing employees to control a variable is also called *self-paced work* (McCormick and Sanders, 1982).

| Epidemiology | Epidemiology is the study of the causes and effects of injuries and illnesses. Epidemiologists working in the area of ergonomics determine whether there are relationships between injuries and the tasks that injured employees were performing. If Mary develops a musculoskeletal problem after performing a certain task day in and day out for ten years, then there is a good likelihood that there is a cause-and-effect relationship between the task and the problem. Table 1.4 contains a list of common cumulative trauma disorders and the tasks that have been found to be associated with these illnesses. |

There are two reasons why employees should be informed about the tasks that have a higher potential for causing injury or illness. First, the employee will be aware that the task is physically stressful and will take adequate precautions when performing it. Second, the employee will be encouraged to suggest how the task can be modified so it is less stressful.

Table 1.4. Common Cumulative Trauma Disorders and Typical Associated Tasks.

Type of Task	Disorder	Occupational Factors
Typing, cashiering	Tension neck Thoracic outlet syndrome Carpal tunnel syndrome	Static or restricted posture, arms abducted or flexed, high-speed finger movement, ulnar deviation
Assembling small parts	Tension neck Thoracic outlet syndrome Wrist tendinitis Epicondylitis	Prolonged restricted posture, forceful ulnar deviation, thumb pressure, repetitive wrist motion, forearm rotation
Packing boxes	Tension neck Carpal tunnel syndrome de Quervain's syndrome	Prolonged load on shoulders, forceful ulnar deviation, repetitive wrist motion
Manual material handling	Thoracic outlet syndrome Shoulder tendinitis	Heavy load on shoulders

Source. Adapted from Putz-Anderson, 1988, p. 22.

Guidelines

The following general guidelines will reduce employees' potential for developing a musculoskeletal injury:

Reduce number of repetitions.
- Schedule activities so the employee does not perform the same motions for more than one hour at a time. For example, if the employee has five hours of typing to do and three hours of copying, schedule his or her day so the activities alternate every hour. Also, give employees the opportunity to schedule their own days.
- Rotate employees performing very repetitious tasks.
- Change the task design so it is less repetitious.

Reduce force.
- Reduce the weight of materials to be lifted or moved.
- Find tools that require the least amount of force to use.

Allow rest.

- Allow employees to perform tasks at their own pace.

- Provide break time commensurate with task intensity.

- Encourage microbreaks. These are short breaks, thirty seconds to one minute long, taken at frequent intervals (every thirty minutes or so) (Donkin, 1989).

Theories of Ergonomics Related to Environment

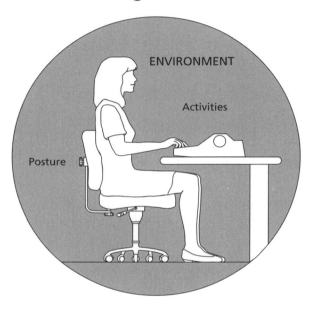

Environmental factors affect people's ability to perform both physical and mental work. The variables that will be briefly discussed here are lighting, thermal factors (heat and cold), noise, and vibration. The information provided here is only an introduction to the effects of these variables, not a complete discussion. Consult an ergonomist or industrial hygienist if you feel you have a workplace problem with heat or cold, noise, or vibration. Also, consult Smith and Kearny (forthcoming) for a discussion of the effects of environmental variables on employees' ability to perform mental work.

Lighting

There can be a number of problems with light in the environment. Two common problems are glare and inadequate light. Glare frequently occurs when light from outside or from room lighting is reflected from the glass on a video display terminal. The results are that the employee cannot see the screen because of the glare and/or the employee experiences eyestrain because of the intensity of the glare. Both results are detrimental to performance.

Lack of adequate lighting can cause conditions such as eyestrain. It can also reduce productivity, because the employee cannot see what he or she needs to do to perform the task.

Thermal environment

Heat does affect an employee's ability to perform work, and it is well known that too much heat can cause heat stroke and heat stress. However, thermal stress below the level that causes heat-related conditions has been shown by Hafez's psychophysical lifting-capacity study (1985) to reduce the amount of weight a subject is willing to lift. Also, the American Conference of Governmental Hygienists found that more rest time is required for workers exposed to higher thermal stress (National Institute of Occupational Safety and Health, 1973). In cold environments, the ergonomic concern is ensuring that enough insulation is provided to protect against the effects of cold.

Noise

The level of noise in an office building varies depending on the types of office machines in use. One personal computer (PC) does not generate enough noise to cause a problem. However, a room that contains several PCs, a couple of copy machines, and a number of busy telephones can get quite noisy. It is well known that high noise can cause hearing loss; however, the effect of lower levels of noise on the ability to perform physical work is much less understood. The Occupational Safety and Health Association (1989) regulates the amount of noise to which employees can be exposed. Therefore, treat potential noise problems seriously.

Vibration

Vibration is probably not a problem for most office workers. However, office workers might be exposed to vibration if their offices are near a production facility or if they use vibrating hand tools like grinders at home. Vibration has been associated with injuries such as Raynaud's syndrome (Gemme, 1987) in which blood flow to the hand is reduced and the fingers feel cold. However, the exact level and magnitude of vibration needed to induce the condition is still unknown. Unfortunately, the effects of whole body vibration are even less well understood.

Guidelines

Environmental variables affect the ability to perform work and may contribute to a musculoskeletal injury. Be aware that lighting, heat, cold, noise, and vibration can cause physical problems and hinder the ability to perform work. This book discusses only lighting in detail. In regard to lighting, follow these general guidelines. Ensure that employees have

- Enough light to perform their tasks
- No glare on their VDTs
- Correct viewing distances from their eyes to their workpieces

Measurable Outcomes of Ergonomically Sound Designs

Redesigning the workplace using ergonomic principles has such measurable outcomes as reduced medical expenses, increased productivity, reduced training costs, and improved morale.

Medical expenses

As was discussed earlier, researchers such as Brogmus and Marko (1992) have found significant medical costs associated with CTDs. However, as other researchers have shown, redesigning workplaces using ergonomic principles can reduce the incidence of musculoskeletal injuries and their associated medical costs.

Productivity

Time and motion studies (Barnes, 1980) have been used since the turn of the century to help improve workplace productivity. Some of the same principles of time and motion studies translate directly into workplace ergonomic improvements. For example, keeping items an employee uses within that employee's normal reach not only improves the speed with which the task can be completed, it also helps prevent employee fatigue.

Training costs

When employees suffer permanent, disabling injuries due to workplace or task design and are no longer able to perform a job, they may be transferred to another task. They must then be trained for the new task, and a new employee must be trained for the task vacated by the injured employee. Incorporating ergonomic principles into the workplace reduces the potential for musculoskeletal injuries and illnesses and keeps employees in the same tasks, thus reducing attrition and its accompanying training costs.

Morale

When employees are injured, morale in a company is reduced (National Safety Council, 1981). News of an injury spreads through a company rapidly, and it may take days before morale improves. Morale is severely affected if more than one employee becomes injured, and low morale affects all parts of the organization. Employees may talk about the incident rather than work, and managers have to take steps to improve morale rather than to manage operations. Prospective employees may even avoid a company if it has a bad reputation in employee safety. All of these results affect company profits. Improving the workplace design decreases injuries and improves morale, and the improvements in morale are seen in the form of increased profits.

Conducting follow-ups with employees, to see that the new designs are in fact working and to make further adjustments if necessary, assures employees that the initial effort was not a one time "program," but a policy to ensure continued improvement in the workplace.

Summary of Key Points

☑ For the past 190 years, U.S. industry has been standardizing its production methods and forcing employees to adapt to the workplace, rather than adapting the workplace to employees' capabilities and limitations. Employees who must adapt to workstations that are not ergonomically designed or adjustable have a greater potential for developing musculoskeletal injuries than employees who are not so constrained.

☑ Training cannot overcome the problems associated with poor workplace design. The workplace needs to be redesigned using the following principles of ergonomics: fit the task or workplace to the individual, design the workplace to fit a range of individuals, and design the workplace to include the individual with the extreme anthropometric dimensions.

☑ The three aspects of work to be considered when designing tasks or workplaces are the posture the employee will have to attain, the activities the employee will have to perform, and the environment in which the employee will work.

Aspect of Ergonomic Design	Design Criteria
Posture	Minimize biochemical stresses.
	Allow easy reach of items.
	Allow ability to shift posture.
Activities	Minimize biomechanical stresses.
	Minimize physiological demands.
	Allow employee to set pace of work.
	Inform employee of physical hazards associated with the task.
Environment	Be aware that lighting, heat, cold, noise, and vibration can cause physical problems and hinder ability to perform.

☑ Improving the workplace reduces medical expenses, improves productivity and morale, and reduces training costs.

SECTION TWO

TECHNIQUES FOR CREATING THE ERGONOMICALLY SOUND WORKPLACE

Overview

What is this section about?

Chapter Two. This chapter contains the procedures you will use to gather ergonomic data on your workplace and organize your ergonomic assessment.

Chapter Three. The procedures in this chapter will determine whether there are mismatches between employees and workstation designs that affect employees' posture. These procedures also provide alternative solutions for correcting any problems detected.

Chapter Four. This chapter contains procedures that improve workplace activities by detecting the risk factors that might contribute to an employee's developing a cumulative trauma disorder from a particular activity. This chapter also provides alternative solutions to any problems detected.

Chapter Five. The procedures in this chapter will help you detect and correct problems in the workplace environment that affect employees' ability to perform physical work.

Chapter Six. One of the most important chapters in this section, even though it is the smallest, this chapter shows you how to schedule and conduct follow-ups to an ergonomic assessment in order to monitor effectiveness.

All Chapters. In addition to the procedures, each chapter contains a decision table to help you select which procedures to perform, the expected results of the procedures, and an annotated bibliography of other good sources of information on the chapter topics. Each procedure contains a purpose statement, a description of when the procedure should be used, a set of terms you may not know, things you should do or items you should obtain before you start, a checklist that takes you through the procedure steps, and an example of the procedure's use.

How is this section organized?

CHAPTER 2

Assessing Workplace Ergonomics

Introduction

The procedures in this chapter show you how to gather data about your workplace as the initial step of an ergonomic assessment. The procedures will give you background on the types of ergonomic problems employees may be having, an overview of the workplace design and the tasks the employees perform, and a model for conducting interviews with the employees and their managers. These procedures should be performed at the start of every ergonomic assessment.

Procedure decision table

The following decision table will help you choose the procedure that applies to your situation.

Procedure	When to Use	Page
2.1. Reviewing Injury and Illness Statistics	To obtain background information as a part of any ergonomic assessment	37
	Periodically to determine if there are musculoskeletal injuries	
2.2. How to Interview a Manager	To gather information during any ergonomic assessment	41
2.3. How to Interview an Employee	To gather information during any ergonomic assessment	45
2.4. Organizing an Ergonomic Assessment	Before conducting the actual assessment of the workplace	49

Results of the procedures in this chapter

After performing the procedures in this chapter, you will have an understanding of the types of injuries and illnesses employees have experienced in a particular workplace, the types of tasks performed in the workplace, and the specific problems employees may be having. You will also be prepared to conduct a well-organized ergonomic assessment of the workplace.

For more information

U.S. Air Force. *U.S. Air Force Guide to Mishap Investigation.* AFP 127-1 Vol I, Washington, D.C., 1987.
A very good source of information on interviewing and incident investigation in general.

Garrett, A. *Interviewing. The Principles and Methods.* New York: Family Service Organization of America, 1972.
A good general source of information on interviewing.

National Safety Council. *Accident Facts.* Chicago, Ill.: National Safety Council, 1990.
A source of information on the number of back injuries and their costs. Data on cumulative trauma disorders is also included but not presented as such so it is hard to dig it out from this book.

U. S. Bureau of Labor Statistics.
Contact the bureau directly for information about the numbers of different types of injuries in a given year (data usually run a couple years behind the present). The address is U.S. Department of Labor, Bureau of Labor Statistics, Office of Safety, Health, and Working Conditions, 601 D Street, N.W., Washington, D.C. 20212.

| **Procedure 2.1** | *Reviewing Injury and Illness Statistics* |

Purpose of this procedure

Reviewing the injury and illness statistics for a given workplace will give you a preliminary understanding of the types of workplace design problems that exist in that workplace and the magnitude of those problems. Because certain types of musculoskeletal injuries are associated with certain types of tasks (see Table 1.4 in Section One), an initial review of injury and illness statistics allows you to focus your assessment on those tasks that may be linked to injuries. Also, you can focus your assessments on those departments or work units with the most problems.

When to use this procedure

The illness and injury statistics review should be performed before any ergonomic assessment is begun. Also, you should review these statistics routinely every six months to determine whether there are trends in the statistics and whether the number of injuries and illnesses of each type is increasing, decreasing, or staying the same. This can tell you whether ergonomic problems are getting worse, better, or staying the same. The information from both the initial review and the subsequent reviews will help you plan your strategies to implement corrective actions.

Terms you may not know

Illness A condition of poor health. Cumulative trauma disorders are usually classified as illnesses.

Injury A physically undesirable condition due to an accident. Back problems are usually classified as injuries.

Lost workday case A severe illness or injury that results in one or more days away from work.

OSHA Form 200 The form that the Occupational Safety and Health Administration (OSHA) requires as a record of workplace injuries and illnesses.

Recordable injury or illness An injury or illness requiring a physician's care.

Restricted activity case An illness or injury so severe that the employee has to be assigned to other tasks because he or she can not perform his or her normal job.

Before you start

Obtain a photocopy of Worksheet A.1 in Resource A. This worksheet is a version of the checklist shown in Exhibit 2.1B.

Also obtain a copy of your company's Occupational Safety and Health Administration (OSHA) Form 200 and any other illness or injury statistical information that is available. Simply call around your organization to find out who the keeper of the OSHA Form 200 is and ask that person for a copy. By law, companies must maintain an OSHA 200 log. However, some companies may be exempt due to their size. Consult 29 CFR 1910 (OSHA, 1989) to determine whether your company is required to maintain an OSHA

Exhibit 2.1A. OSHA Form 200.

U.S. Department of Labor

Bureau of Labor Statistics
Log and Summary of Occupational
Injuries and Illnesses

NOTE: This form is required by Public Law 91-596 and must be kept in the establishment for 5 years. Failure to maintain and post can result in the issuance of citations and assessment of penalties. (See posting requirements on the other side of form.)

RECORDABLE CASES: You are required to record information about every occupational death; every nonfatal occupational illness; and those nonfatal occupational injuries which involve one or more of the following: loss of consciousness, restriction of work or motion, transfer to another job, or medical treatment (other than first aid). (See definitions on the other side of form.)

Company Name _____
Establishment Name _____
Establishment Address _____

For Calendar Year 19____   Page ____ of ____

(A) Case or File Number	(B) Date of Injury or Onset of Illness Mo./day/	(C) Employee's Name	(D) Occupation	(E) Department	(F) Description of Injury or Illness	Injury Related (1)	(2)	(3)	(4) DAYS away	(5) DAYS restricted	(6) Injuries Without Lost Workdays	Illness Related (8)	Occupational skin (a)	Dust diseases of lungs (b)	Respiratory poisoning (c)	Poisoning (d)	Disorders toxic agents (e)	Disorders physical agents (f)	Disorders repeated trauma (e)	All other occupational illnesses (g)	(9)	(10)	(11) DAYS away	(12) DAYS restricted	(13) Illness Without Lost Workdays
1	1/2/93	Typist	Typing	cut finger							✓														
2	2/5/93	"	"	tendonitis															✓						✓
3	3/2/93	"	"	carpal tunnel syndrome															✓						✓
4	4/6/93	"	"	back sprain																	✓	2	8		
5	5/10/93	"	"	bruised ankle		✓		2																	
6	6/5/93	"	"	carpal tunnel syndrome															✓		✓	10			
7	7/5/93	"	"	epicondylitis																	✓	3	10		
8	8/5/93	"	"	cut finger							✓														
9	10/15/93	"	"	foreign item in eye							✓														
10	11/26/93	"	"	back sprain																	✓	20	50		

PREVIOUS PAGE TOTALS →

TOTALS (Instructions on other side of form) →

Certification of Annual Summary Totals By _____   Title _____   Date _____

OSHA No. 200

POST ONLY THIS PORTION OF THE LAST PAGE NO LATER THAN FEBRUARY 1.

38   SECTION TWO

200 log. Exhibit 2.1A is an example of a completed 200 form. Keep in mind that OSHA forms are sometimes changed, so ensure that your 200 form is the current version required by law.

Usually, the safety or human relations department maintains the OSHA Form 200, and it should not be a problem for you to review it, because, again by law, it has to be posted during the month of February, after the end of the calendar year. However, the names of the injured are kept confidential, and so the keeper of the log may cover the names or ask you to keep the names confidential. The injuries and illnesses listed on the log are only those classified as OSHA recordables, that is, they were serious enough to require a physician's treatment.

Your organization may also keep a file of less serious injuries, classified as first aid cases. The information contained in this file is usually not as well organized as that on the OSHA Form 200 and may or may not be of help to you.

What to do

After you obtain the OSHA Form 200, review the information to determine the types of injuries that have occurred in the workplace, the departments and the occupations of the employees who have experienced musculoskeletal injuries or illnesses, and the relative magnitude of these problems. Once you have this information, you can focus your ergonomic assessment on the most severe problems first. Exhibit 2.1B shows a checklist that will guide you through your review.

Example of procedure use

Elizabeth was tasked by her boss to determine whether their company was having any workplace design problems. Elizabeth had heard rumors that employees were complaining of problems, but she needed to find out if anyone had actually been injured as a result of workplace design. She obtained a copy of the company's OSHA Form 200 from the safety department. Ten injuries and illnesses were listed on the form (see Exhibit 2.1A). Using the injury and illness statistics review procedure and the information in Table 1.1, Elizabeth determined that injuries and illnesses 2, 3, 4, 6, 7, and 10 were possibly due to workplace design and that the injured employees were typists or data entry people. She noted this information on Worksheet A.1. Elizabeth next determined how many days away from work and days of restricted activity there were. Illnesses 4, 6, 7, and 10 had resulted in 103 days away from work or days of restricted activity, and she also noted this total. Elizabeth next determined the relative rate of injuries and illnesses involving days away from work and days of restricted activity. The company employed a total of four hundred typists and forty data entry personnel. She estimated the rate as one injury or illness per one hundred employees for the typists and one injury or illness per twenty employees for the data entry personnel. She reported these numbers to her boss and prepared to begin interviewing the employees and managers.

Exhibit 2.1B. Checklist for Reviewing Injury and Illness Statistics.

Step	Review Checklist	Yes	No	How to Do Step
1.	Are there musculoskeletal injuries or illnesses listed in column F of the OSHA Form 200? If yes, note the injury or illness, department, and occupation of the employee in the space provided on worksheet A.1.	☐	☐	Table 1.1 in Section One lists the common musculoskeletal injuries. Back strains and sprains and injuries to the vertebral discs are also considered musculoskeletal injuries. If the injury appears on this Table or is a back injury, then the answer to the question is yes. If column f under "Type of Illness" on Form 200 is checked, then that illness should also be included in your review.
2.	Did the injuries or illnesses require days away from work or days of restricted activity? If yes, determine how many days away from work or days of restricted work there were for each musculoskeletal injury or illness and note it in the space provided on worksheet A.1. To determine total days add the number of days in columns 4, 5, 11, and 12 on OSHA Form 200.	☐	☐	Column 2 on OSHA Form 200 will be checked if the problem was classified as an injury; column 9 will be checked if the problem was classified as an illness. Note that in general days away from work indicate a more serious condition.
3.	Determine the total number of employees who work in each of the departments and perform the occupations that appear on the OSHA form.	☐	☐	Call the respective departmental managers to obtain this information.
4.	Divide the total number of employees who perform the occupation by the total number of injuries and illnesses that involve days away from work or days of restricted activity, and enter the result on the worksheet. The result estimates a musculoskeletal injury and illness rate. Repeat the procedure for the injuries and illnesses that did not involve restricted days or days away from work.	☐	☐	For example, if there are 20 typists and 2 injuries then 20/2 = 10, or 1 injury per 10 employees. Compare the rates for the injuries and illnesses to decide which tasks need ergonomic attention first.

Procedure 2.2 — How to Interview a Manager

Purpose of this procedure

Interviews with managers are important to ergonomic assessments because managers typically possess information that can improve your initial understanding of potential workplace design problems. Indeed, a wealth of information can be obtained if the manager to be interviewed has had good relations with his or her employees. However, little or no information will be gained if the manager does not get along with employees.

When to use this procedure

This procedure should be routinely performed as a part of any workplace ergonomic assessment. You should also perform this procedure if employees begin complaining about a particular workplace. If you are the workplace manager, use this procedure as an outline to help you understand your own potential workplace problems.

Terms you may not know

Open-ended question   A question that cannot be answered with just a yes or a no. For example, "What types of problems are employees having?" is an open-ended question. "Do employees have problems?" is not an open-ended question.

Before you start

Obtain a photocopy of Worksheet B.1 in Resource B. This worksheet is a version of the checklist in Exhibit 2.2A.

You will need to make arrangements for a comfortable, private place in which to interview the manager. Also, ensure that the time you arrange for the interview is convenient to the manager. Explain to the manager that the information will be used for the employees' benefit and that the results will benefit the manager in the future by reducing his or her costs. We all know the jokes about being wary of the person who says, "I am from the government [or upper level management], and I'm here to help you," and some managers may not welcome your activity at first, but by being sincere about the activity, you can develop a rapport with the manager.

What to do

The procedure shown in Exhibit 2.2A determines what tasks the employees perform and gives an initial picture of any problems the employees are having, the aspects of the workplace causing the problems, and whether the employees have experienced any musculoskeletal injuries or illnesses. The information you obtain in this interview will be used in subsequent procedures.

Exhibit 2.2A. Checklist for Interviewing a Manager.

Step	Interview Checklist	Yes	No	How to Do Step
1.	Determine and then describe the types of tasks the employees perform:	☐	☐	Use the list provided here to help you determine the tasks. Ask open-ended questions about these tasks so you obtain the most information possible.
	Office tasks			
	Typing	☐	☐	
	Filing	☐	☐	
	Letter stuffing	☐	☐	
	Proofreading	☐	☐	
	Photocopying	☐	☐	
	Bench work with light repair and assembly			
	Placing circuit boards in computers	☐	☐	
	Handling objects weighing less than twenty pounds	☐	☐	
	Using primarily the hands and wrists to perform the motions in the assembly or repair	☐	☐	
	Working in a fast food restaurant	☐	☐	
	Bench work with heavy assembly or repair			
	Assembling objects weighing over twenty pounds	☐	☐	
	Using the elbows and shoulders to perform the motions used in the assembly or repair	☐	☐	
	Light lifting: lifting only a few containers in a day	☐	☐	
	Heavy lifting: lifting numerous containers in a day	☐	☐	
	Manufacturing: operating milling machines, lathes, tools weighing over twenty pounds	☐	☐	
	Heavy service industries			
	Servicing cars, trucks, and buses	☐	☐	
	Working in cafeterias	☐	☐	
	Working in laundries	☐	☐	
2.	What types of workstations are used in the workplace:			
	Standing	☐	☐	
	Sitting	☐	☐	
	With VDT	☐	☐	
3.	Ask the manager to describe the workstation and/or workplace and record the description on the worksheet.	☐	☐	Use open-ended questions to get a full description of the workstation and/or workplace.

Step	Interview Checklist	Yes	No	How to Do Step
4.	Ask the manager to discuss any employee complaints of pain, discomfort, or other problems, and determine the body parts where employees are experiencing pain or discomfort:			Use open-ended questions and the list provided to encourage full discussion.
	Neck	☐	☐	
	Shoulder	☐	☐	
	Upper back	☐	☐	
	Lower back	☐	☐	
	Elbow/forearm	☐	☐	
	Hand/wrist	☐	☐	
	Fingers	☐	☐	
	Thigh/knee	☐	☐	
	Lower leg	☐	☐	
	Ankle/foot	☐	☐	
5.	Ask the manager to list any specific complaints the employee might be having with the following environmental factors:			Use open-ended questions and the list provided to determine specific complaints.
	Lighting	☐	☐	
	Glare on computer screen	☐	☐	
	Noise	☐	☐	
	Thermal environment	☐	☐	
	Vibration	☐	☐	
	Lack of adequate space	☐	☐	
	Workplace furniture (benches, chairs, desks) that causes postural stress	☐	☐	
6.	Have there been any recent changes in the workplace that might have affected employees' ability to perform work? If yes, determine what has changed recently and describe it on the worksheet.	☐	☐	Sometimes what appear to be little changes in the workplace can have a significant impact on employees. When only part of the work system is changed and not the whole system, the work system may be thrown out of balance, causing problems for the employees.

Exhibit 2.2A. (Continued)

Step	Interview Checklist	Yes	No	How to Do Step
7.	Do any employees use sick time for back pain or other musculoskeletal problems? If yes, list the problems on the worksheet.	☐	☐	An employee who appears to use excessive amounts of sick time might have a musculoskeletal injury or illness, but for one reason or another, he or she does not want to report it as an occupational problem. Sick time can be a touchy subject, so tread lightly.
8.	Determine what the manager feels are the reasons for the employees' complaints and list the reasons on the worksheet.			
9.	Tour the facility with the manager in order to get a feel for the magnitude of the task, get initial impressions of the types of problems employees may be having, and give employees the opportunity to begin to know you. Determine the following from your tour: Is the workplace clean and orderly? Does the lighting appear adequate? Does the workplace feel too hot or cold? Does the workplace sound too noisy? Are employees exposed to vibration?	 ☐ ☐ ☐ ☐ ☐	 ☐ ☐ ☐ ☐ ☐	Select a time that operations will be as normal as possible and the employees will be available. Ask the manager to introduce you to the employees.

Example of procedure use

Michelle had begun to perform an ergonomic assessment of the employees of the nursing home where she was employed as director of operations. She completed Procedure 2.1 and found that the employees in the cafeteria had experienced a number of musculoskeletal injuries during the past year. In fact, the rate was one injury per fifteen employees. Michelle debated whether to perform Procedure 2.2, since she was the manager, but decided to go ahead in order to get an initial understanding of problems in the cafeteria. As she performed the procedure, she found that it did help her understand the cafeteria better. She determined that the tasks were primarily done standing and that the employees took much more sick time than the other employees she supervised. She also noted all the employees' complaints about the cafeteria over the past year. As Michelle conducted the walk-around of the cafeteria, the employees asked her questions about what she was doing and appeared very interested in helping her determine what needed to be fixed to improve their working conditions.

| **Procedure 2.3** | ***How to Interview an Employee*** |

Purpose of this procedure

Interviews with employees are important because the information obtained from them provides the most important insights into the ergonomics of the workplace. You will gain understanding of the types of problems employees may be experiencing, which will help you focus your assessment. Also, employees may have ideas about how their problems can be resolved.

When to use this procedure

Employee interviews should be routinely performed as a part of any workplace ergonomic assessment. Every employee whose workplace is to be assessed should be interviewed. This procedure should also be performed when employees come to you with complaints about their workstations or workplaces.

Terms you may not know

Open-ended question A question that cannot be answered with just a yes or a no. For example, What types of problems are employees having? is an open-ended question. Do employees have problems? is not an open-ended question.

Before you start

Obtain a photocopy of Worksheet B.2 in Resource B. This worksheet is a version of the checklist in Exhibit 2.3A.

Arrange for a comfortable, private place to interview each employee. Be sure that you have talked to each employee's manager and that the manager knows and agrees with your procedure and does not think the employee is going over the manager's head. Having the manager's buy-in to the assessment is as important as having each employee's buy-in.

What to do

Interview each employee to determine if he or she is experiencing workplace-related problems, and use open-ended questions as you did in the manager interview in order to get full answers. The information you obtain will be needed in subsequent procedures. Part of your job is to phrase your questions in a manner each employee will understand. This may not be an easy task, and you may have to interview an employee several times to get all the information you need. Also, keep in mind that an employee may know the solution to any problem he or she is experiencing.

Above all else, to be sure that the employee gives you the information about the workplace that only the employee knows, do not talk down to any employee. It is also important to wear clothes that match the culture of the workplace. For example, if the employee will be dressed casually, you should not come dressed for the interview in a three-piece suit or your most tailored outfit. Also, if during the course of the interview you agree to do something for the employee be sure to follow through and do it. Nothing defeats trust more than promising things that you cannot deliver. Agree to do what you can, but do not promise the world.

Exhibit 2.3A. Checklist for Interviewing an Employee.

Step	Interview Checklist	Yes	No	How to Do Step
1.	Is the employee experiencing any musculoskeletal problems? If no, go to step 2. If yes, perform steps 1a, 1b, 1c, 1d, and 1e.	☐	☐	Explain to the employee what musculoskeletal injuries are, and use the body diagrams in Worksheet B.2 to help the employee identify any problems.
1a.	Ask the employee to indicate his or her problem areas on the body diagrams in Worksheet B.2.			
1b.	Determine the type of physical symptoms the employee is having, including aching, burning, color loss, cramping, numbness ("asleep"), pain, stiffness, swelling, tingling, weakness, or other symptoms. Enter this information as the "problem type" in the appropriate box on the body diagram in Worksheet B.2.			This information can be useful when discussing the employee's problem with a physician.
1c.	Ask the employee to indicate the relative severity of the problem on a scale from 1 to 10, with 1 being a minimal problem and 10 being unbearable. Enter this rating as the "severity" in the appropriate box on the body diagram.			This information is useful for both medical discussions and for prioritizing your assessments so that you evaluate the workplaces of the employees with the most severe problems first.
1d.	Has the employee sought medical attention for the problem either from the company physician or a private physician? If no, encourage the employee to see the company physician, or a private physician if there is no company physician. If yes, ask what the doctor said.	☐	☐	Employees may not always divulge this information. So do not assume everything is fine just because an employee does not respond to this question or leads you to assume the answer is no. This is a touchy area also—probing into personal matters at work can cause problems—so you may want to involve your safety department, company physician, or human resources department.

Step	Interview Checklist	Yes	No	How to Do Step
1e.	Does the employee have an idea about what is causing the problem? If yes, note the employees' idea on the worksheet and use it as the starting point of the assessment.	☐	☐	Employees know their workplace better than anybody else. They may have the perfect solution to the problem. Their solution, however, may not be voiced in terms you immediately understand, so work with employees until you do understand this solution.
2.	Does the employee have trouble reaching needed items in the workplace?	☐	☐	
3.	Does the employee have any difficulty attaining and staying in the postures required by the workplace?	☐	☐	
4.	Does the employee like the way his or her workstation is arranged?	☐	☐	
5.	Does the employee feel cramped in his or her workplace?	☐	☐	
6.	Can the employee attain a full range of motion in his or her workplace?	☐	☐	
7.	Does the employee have to lift items in his or her workplace?	☐	☐	
8.	Does the employee have problems with any of the following: Lighting levels Glare on a computer screen Noise Temperature of the workplace Vibration	☐	☐	

For items 8 (Glare on a computer screen, Noise, Temperature of the workplace, Vibration):

	Yes	No
Glare on a computer screen	☐	☐
Noise	☐	☐
Temperature of the workplace	☐	☐
Vibration	☐	☐

Exhibit 2.3A. (Continued)

Step	Interview Checklist	Yes	No	How to Do Step
9.	Has the employee had training on any of the following:	☐	☐	
	The causes of cumulative trauma disorders			
	The causes of back injuries	☐	☐	
	The benefits of microbreaks	☐	☐	
	How to perform stretching exercises	☐	☐	
	How to adjust his or her workstation and/or chair	☐	☐	
	If the answer to any of the items in step 9 is yes, does the employee feel the training was adequate?	☐	☐	

Example of procedure use

Jennifer was an internal auditor for a Pacific Northwest mining operation. She has three accountants working for her including Steve, a new hire who had been with the company for about six months. Steve complained a lot, but he also normally posed a solution to the problem after first voicing the complaint loudly. When he complained that his desk was a piece of junk and was causing him back problems, Jennifer heard the complaint and asked him into her office. Since this complaint dealt with his health, Jennifer knew she had to take him seriously.

She decided to use Procedure 2.3 to help her find out what the problem was. She explained to Steve what she was going to do, and she began the interview with an open-ended question: "Tell me, Steve, what is wrong with your workplace?" Steven went into great detail about all the problems he was having with his workstation, but he focused especially on the fact that his desk was too low and it forced him to lean forward too much. Steve was tall and a desk of normal height did not fit him well. Jennifer took down all the information on Worksheet B.2. After Steve was done talking, she asked him what could be changed to correct the problem. Steve said simply, "I need my desk raised." Jennifer told Steve she would find him another desk and would do so in the next couple of weeks. She kept her word. She also followed up on the result using the procedure described in Chapter Six.

| Procedure 2.4 | **Organizing the Ergonomic Assessment** |

Purpose of this procedure

The purpose of this procedure is to help you organize the ergonomic assessment of the workplace. At this point you have

- Reviewed the injury and illness statistics
- Interviewed the manager of the department or organizational unit
- Interviewed the employees

Now you need to decide which additional procedures to perform and/or whether to call an ergonomic specialist for help. This procedure will help you make these decisions.

When to use this procedure

This procedure is performed as a routine part of all ergonomic assessments.

Before you start

1. Assemble your worksheets from your review of the injury and illness statistics and your interviews with managers and employees.

2. Obtain a copy of Worksheet C.1 in Resource C. This worksheet is a version of the checklist in Exhibit 2.4A.

What to do

You have gathered some data about the workplace. Now you have to decide whether you can tackle the job yourself, and if so, what procedure you should use. The steps for this decision procedure are shown in Exhibit 2.4A.

Exhibit 2.4A. Checklist for Organizing the Ergonomic Assessment.

Step	Organization Checklist	Yes	No	How to Do Step
1.	Check that you have data in all the areas in the following list. Seek help from an ergonomic specialist if you have a problem in an area marked with an asterisk.			If there is an area in which you do not have data, you will have to perform the appropriate procedure (2.1, 2.2, and/or 2.3) to produce the necessary data.
	Postures			
	Standing	☐	☐	
	Sitting	☐	☐	
	With VDT	☐	☐	
	Activities			
	Office tasks			
	Typing	☐	☐	
	Filing	☐	☐	
	Letter stuffing	☐	☐	
	Proofreading	☐	☐	
	Photocopying	☐	☐	
	Bench work with light repair and assembly			
	Placing circuit boards in computers	☐	☐	
	Handling objects weighing less than twenty pounds	☐	☐	
	Using primarily the hands and wrists to perform the motions in the assembly or repair	☐	☐	
	Working in a fast food restaurant	☐	☐	
	Bench work with heavy assembly or repair			
	Assembling objects weighing over twenty pounds	☐	☐	
	Using the elbows and shoulders to perform the motions used in the assembly or repair	☐	☐	
	Light lifting: lifting only a few containers in a day	☐	☐	
	Heavy lifting: lifting numerous containers in a day	☐	☐	
	Manufacturing: operating milling machines, lathes, tools weighing over twenty pounds	☐	☐	
	Heavy service industries			
	Servicing cars, trucks, and buses	☐	☐	
	Working in cafeterias	☐	☐	
	Working laundries	☐	☐	

Step	Organization Checklist	Yes	No	How to Do Step
	Specific activities problems			
	Lack of adequate space	☐	☐	
	Problems with workplace layout	☐	☐	
	Many hand and upper-extremity activities	☐	☐	
	Environment			
	Lighting	☐	☐	
	Glare on computer screens	☐	☐	
	Noise	☐	☐	
	Thermal environment	☐	☐	
	Vibration	☐	☐	
2.	Judging from your initial assessment of the problems, does an ergonomic specialist need to be consulted? If yes, list on Worksheet C.1 the areas in which a specialist is needed.	☐	☐	
3.	On the worksheet, describe the types of workplaces and all the problems the ergonomic assessment will examine.			
4.	Use the data you have collected and Table 2.4A to decide which procedures to perform for which workstations. Enter the information on the worksheet.			
5.	Schedule your assessments with the manager and the employees to ensure that everyone will be available and that the employees will be performing the tasks to be assessed at the scheduled time.			

Table 2.4A. Master Procedure Decision Table.

At This Workplace Location	With This Problem	Use Procedure Number
Sitting workstation with VDT	Employee in awkward posture	3.1
	Employee's elbow joint not at 90 degrees	3.1
	Employee's wrists deviated when typing	3.1
	Employee has musculoskeletal injury	3.1
	Employee complains about workstation	3.1
Sitting workstation without VDT	Employee in awkward posture	3.2
	Employee's wrists or shoulders deviated	3.2
	Employee has musculoskeletal injury	3.2
	Employee complains about workstation	3.2
Workstation chairs	Chair not adjustable to accommodate employee	3.3
	Employee's legs fall asleep	3.3
	You are preparing to buy new chairs	3.3
	Employee complains about chair	3.3
Standing workstation with a VDT	Employee in stooped posture	3.5
	Employee's wrists deviated when typing	3.5
	Employee has musculoskeletal injury	3.5
	Employee complains about workstation	3.5

At This Workplace Location	With This Problem	Use Procedure Number
Desk at a sitting workstation	Current desk does not accommodate employee	3.4
	You are preparing to buy new desks	3.4
	Employee complains about desk	3.4
Standing workstation without a VDT	Employee in stooped posture	3.6
	Employee's wrists or shoulders deviated	3.6
	Employee has musculoskeletal injury	3.6
	Employee complains about workstation	3.6
Workbenches for a standing workstation	Workbench cannot be adjusted to accommodate employee	3.7
	You are preparing to buy new workbenches	3.7
Any workstation	Employee must lean forward to grab objects	4.1
	Employee appears cramped for space	4.1
	Employee's wrists or shoulders are deviated	4.1
	Employee has upper-extremity musculoskeletal injury	4.1
	Employee performs highly repetitive tasks	4.2
	You are preparing to buy an ergonomic gadget such as a wrist rest or arm support	4.3

Table 2.4A. (Continued)

At This Workplace Location	With This Problem	Use Procedure Number
Any place lifting tasks may occur	Lifting is not a normal part of employee's job	4.4
	Employee has infrequent lifting tasks	4.4
	Office employee has lifting tasks	4.4
Any place adequate lighting may be an issue	Lighting is poor	5.1
	Lighting is uneven	5.1
	Viewing distance may be inappropriate for employee	5.1
	Employee has glare on VDT	5.2
Workplace as a whole	Follow-up required on ergonomic assessments	6.1

Posture: Creating and Maintaining Healthy Body Alignment

Introduction

This chapter is designed to help you improve employees' postures at both sitting and standing workstations with or without video display terminals (VDTs). You will learn how to recognize good and bad postures, adjust existing workstations to fit employees, and select new chairs and workstations. Only certain of these procedures will be performed, depending on the type of workplace you are assessing.

Procedure decision table

The following decision table will help you choose the procedure that applies to your situation if you have not already completed this step in Procedure 2.4.

Procedure	When to Use	Page
3.1. Assessing a Sitting Workstation with VDT	Employee in awkward posture	58
	Employee's elbow joint not at 90 degrees	
	Employee's wrists deviated when typing	
	Employee has musculoskeletal injury	
	Employee complains about workstation	
3.2. Assessing a Sitting Workstation Without VDT	Employee in awkward posture	64
	Employee's wrists or shoulders deviated	
	Employee has musculoskeletal injury	
	Employee complains about workstation	

What are the results of the procedures in this chapter?

The procedures in this chapter focus on adjusting workstations to fit employees so these employees can attain good sitting and standing postures. Using these procedures to adjust your employees' workstations will improve employee performance by reducing muscle fatigue, optimizing the relationship between the employee and the workplace, and ultimately reducing the incidence of musculoskeletal injuries.

For more information

Grandjean, E. *Ergonomics in Computerized Offices.* Bristol, Pa.: Taylor and Francis, 1987.
  An excellent book on office ergonomics, although the information is presented from an ergonomist's point of view. Includes information on chair design, workplace layout, and workstation design.

Meister, D. *Behavioral Analysis and Measurement Methods.* New York: Wiley, 1985.
  A good reference for assistance in performing link analyses and task analysis in general.

National Institute for Occupational Safety and Health. *The Industrial Environment: Its Evaluation and Control.* Washington, D.C.: U.S. Government Printing Office, 1973.
  Geared toward the industrial hygiene aspects of workplaces, this work has some valuable information on lighting.

Rodgers, S. H. *Ergonomic Design for People at Work.* Belmont, Calif.: Lifetime Learning Publications, 1983.
  A Kodak publication that has very good information about workplace design from an industrial point of view.

Van Cott, H. P., and Kinkade, R. G. *Human Engineering Guide to Equipment Design.* New York: McGraw-Hill, 1972.
  A good source of information on anthropometry.

| Procedure 3.1 | Assessing a Sitting Workstation with VDT |

Purpose of this procedure

The correct adjustment of a sitting workstation with a video display terminal (VDT) is one of the best methods of preventing an employee from developing a musculoskeletal injury or illness. This procedure provides you with a set of steps for adjusting sitting VDT workstations to meet the individual physical needs of each employee. In addition to preventing certain illnesses and injuries, a properly adjusted workstation also helps employees perform at their optimal level by reducing their fatigue and improving the workplace layouts so that they can work more efficiently.

When to use this procedure

Optimally, this procedure should be performed for every employee who works at a sitting VDT workstation; however, this is not always possible. The following indicators should alert you to an employee's need for an ergonomic assessment:

- The employee has experienced a musculoskeletal injury or illness and/or complains about aches and pains at work.

- Several employees in a work unit have experienced musculoskeletal injuries or illnesses while working at similar workstations.

- The employee is observed sitting in an awkward posture:

    The employee's elbows are not bent at a ninety-degree angle.

    The employee's wrists are deviated.

    The employee is leaning forward.

    The employee looks uncomfortable.

    The employee's feet are not supported.

- The employee complains that the workstation is not comfortable.

- The employee's work output is dropping off, and he or she is reporting in sick more often than normal.

- The employee avoids his or her workstation and gravitates toward other employees' offices or conducts work at other locations in the building.

Terms you may not know

Arm support A device that typically attaches to the workstation or desk in order to support the forearm (see Figure 4.3A).

Deviated When applied to the posture of the upper extremities, particularly the wrists or shoulders, this term means these parts of the body are not in a neutral posture. (Figure 1.5 on page 17 shows the neutral and deviated wrists postures and Figure 4.2A on page 105 shows neutral and deviated shoulder postures.)

Monitor arm A jointed arm-like device on which a computer monitor is placed to give it a great degree of adjustability.

Normal cone of vision The field within which the eye can easily rotate to see objects.

Wrist rest A device, usually a bar of firm foam rubber, placed under the wrists to keep them in a neutral posture (see Figure 3.1).

Figure 3.1. Wrist Rest.

Wrist rest

Before you start

Before you conduct an ergonomic assessment of a sitting workstation, complete the following steps:

1. Familiarize yourself with Figure 3.1A, illustrating good posture at a sitting workstation with a VDT.

2. Make arrangements with the manager and the employee to conduct the assessment.

3. Ensure buy-in from the employee.

4. Obtain a yardstick and a twelve-inch ruler.

5. Obtain a photocopy of Worksheet D.1 in Resource D. This worksheet is a version of the checklist in Exhibit 3.1A.

What to do

Figure 3.1A shows the fundamentals of good posture at a sitting VDT workstation. The checklist for this procedure (Exhibit 3.1A) takes you through the steps of assessing and adjusting the workstation until the employee can attain a proper sitting posture, as depicted in this figure. There is no one best way of adjusting a sitting workstation because everyone's body dimensions are different. Therefore, this procedure presents several options for adjusting the workstation. Once the employee is adjusted to a proper sitting posture, he or she will feel comfortable; so talk to employees about how they feel as you manipulate the various components of their workstations. You may have to perform several iterations of the steps in the checklist before the workstation will be properly adjusted to the employee.

The numbers of the steps in the checklist correspond to the numbers of the descriptions in Figure 3.1A.

Figure 3.1A. Fundamentals of Good Posture at a Sitting Workstation with a VDT.

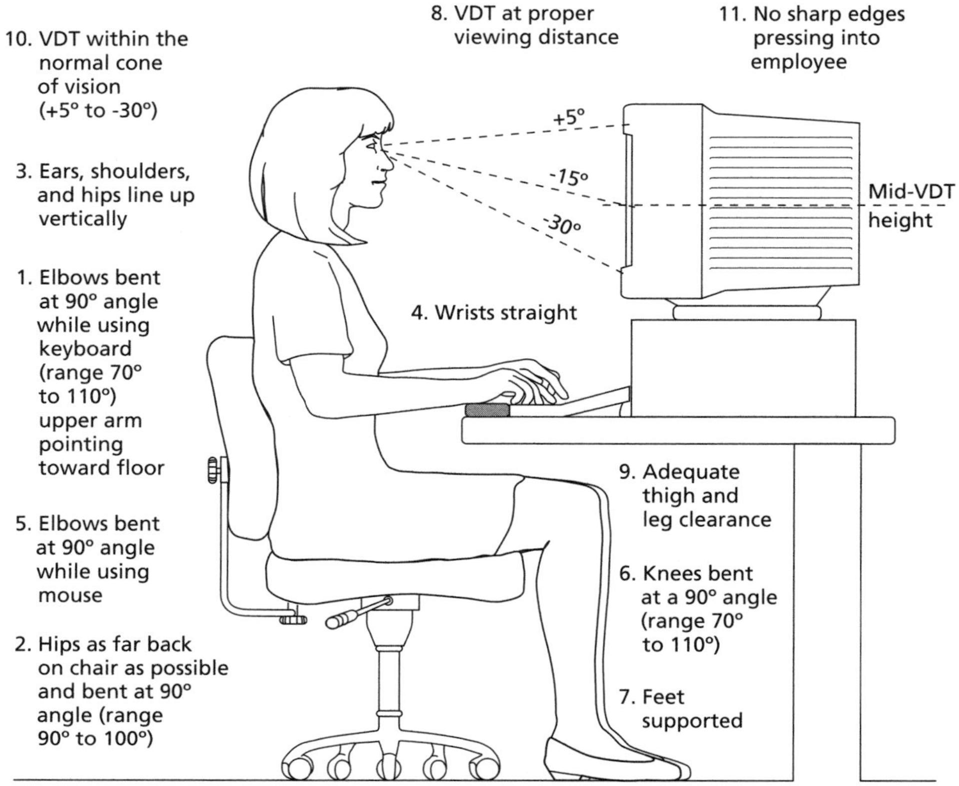

10. VDT within the normal cone of vision (+5° to -30°)

8. VDT at proper viewing distance

11. No sharp edges pressing into employee

3. Ears, shoulders, and hips line up vertically

+5°
-15°
-30°

Mid-VDT height

1. Elbows bent at 90° angle while using keyboard (range 70° to 110°) upper arm pointing toward floor

4. Wrists straight

5. Elbows bent at 90° angle while using mouse

9. Adequate thigh and leg clearance

6. Knees bent at a 90° angle (range 70° to 110°)

2. Hips as far back on chair as possible and bent at 90° angle (range 90° to 100°)

7. Feet supported

Source: Adapted from Grandjean, 1987; American National Standards Institute/Human Factors Society, 1988; and Putz-Anderson, 1988.

Example of procedure use

Bob, who was Judy's colleague, noticed that Judy was in an extremely awkward-looking posture in relation to her computer desk. When he asked her if she liked the way she was sitting, she told him she didn't and went on to say that she felt her keyboard was too high. Bob asked Judy to wait a minute while he got his copy of Procedure 3.1. As he performed step 1, Bob found that Judy's elbows were at an angle of much less than ninety degrees although her upper arm was in the correct posture. When he asked Judy to raise her chair to correct the elbow posture, she told him she didn't know how to adjust her chair, so he showed her. Simply raising her chair brought Judy into a correct posture in relation to her workstation.

Exhibit 3.1A. Checklist for Assessing a Sitting Workstation with VDT.

Step	Assessment Checklist	Yes	No	How to Do Step
1.	Is the elbow joint bent at approximately a 90° angle while the employee is using the keyboard (the angle can range from 70° to 110°)? If no, adjust the chair height and/or keyboard height. If they can not be adjusted, try a different chair and/or desk. Most companies have a storage area that is a good source of old furniture. Consider buying a different chair or desk if there is no other way to achieve the correct elbow angle.	☐	☐	Eyeball the employee's elbow joint to determine if it is bent at about a 90° angle. You can also hold the corner of a square piece of cardboard up to the joint to compare the 90° angle of the corner to the angle of the elbow.
2.	Is the hip joint bent at approximately a 90° angle (the angle can range from 90° to 100°)? If no, adjust the chair height or try a different chair.	☐	☐	Eyeball the hip joint to determine if it is bent at a 90° angle.
3.	Are the ears, shoulders, and hips lined up vertically (the head can be tipped slightly forward at a comfortable angle of 5° to 10°)? If no, adjust the chair height, the angle of the backrest, the viewing distance to the VDT (see Procedure 5.1), or the keyboard height.	☐	☐	Step back from the employee and look at his or her seated posture. You should be able to draw an imaginary straight line pointed down from their ears through their shoulders and hips.
4.	Are the wrists straight? If no, adjust the chair height or the keyboard height. Try a different chair and/or desk if the workstation cannot be properly adjusted. Also, consider using a wrist rest (see Procedure 4.3).	☐	☐	Look at the wrists to determine if they are straight or deviated. Compare the wrist posture to that in Figure 1.5 in Section One.
5.	Is a mouse used at the workstation? If yes, perform steps 5a, 5b, and 5c.	☐	☐	

Exhibit 3.1A. (Continued)

Step	Assessment Checklist	Yes	No	How to Do Step
5a.	Is the elbow bent at a 90° angle while the employee is using the mouse (the angle can range from 70° to 110°)? If no, move the mouse closer to the person. An arm support can also be used (see Procedure 4.3).	☐	☐	Eyeball the elbow to determine if it appears to be bent at approximately a 90° angle (see step 1 for an additional method of determining the angle).
5b.	Is the upper arm close to the body? If no, move the mouse closer to the person.	☐	☐	Look to see that the upper arm is close to the body and not abducted (pulled away).
5c.	Is the wrist deviated? If yes, adjust the height of the mouse and/or use a wrist rest (see Procedure 4.3).	☐	☐	Look at the wrist to determine whether it is deviated either to the left or right, up or down.
6.	Are the knees bent at a 90° angle (the angle can range from 70° to 110°)? If no, adjust the chair height or try a different chair.	☐	☐	Again, just eyeball the knee joint and determine if it is bent at a 90° angle.
7.	Are the feet supported? If no, give the employee a footrest because at this point the workstation has been adjusted for the employee's elbows, hips, wrists, and knees.	☐	☐	This is an easy one. Look to see if the feet are flat on the floor.
8.	Is the VDT at the proper viewing distance (approximately the employee's arm length)? If no, adjust the distance of the monitor from the employee's eyes, moving the monitor forward or back until it is positioned correctly. A monitor arm can help you achieve the correct position.	☐	☐	Ask the employee to sit in his or her optimal posture and reach for the screen. The employee should be able to reach the screen without bending forward. At the same time, ask the employee if he or she has any difficulty seeing the screen. You may need to ensure that the lighting levels are correct (see Procedure 5.1).

Step	Assessment Checklist	Yes	No	How to Do Step
9.	Is there adequate thigh and leg clearance? If no, try a desk with a thinner desktop to provide more leg clearance. Remove items stored underneath the desk.	☐	☐	The employee needs to be as close to the work as possible. A desktop that is too thick or items stored under the desk can prevent the employee from getting close to the desk. Ask the employee to sit at the workstation. Look to see that there are no obstacles to a good posture.
10.	Is the part of the screen the employee uses most within the normal cone of vision, which is +5° (above the horizontal axis) to −30° (below the horizontal axis)? If no, adjust the height of the VDT by removing the monitor base if the monitor is too high or adding a monitor base if the monitor is too low. A monitor arm can also be used to raise or lower the VDT.	☐	☐	The mid-VDT height should be about 8 inches below the employee's eye height. You can measure this by holding a yardstick horizontally at the employee's eye level. At the point where the yardstick bisects the monitor, use a shorter ruler to measure 8 inches down.
11.	Are any sharp edges pressing into the employee? If yes, pad the items that are causing problems with light foam rubber or remove them.	☐	☐	Look at the employee sitting at the workstation to determine if the edge of the desk, the keyboard, or other items at the workstation are pressing into the employee's flesh. Such pressure can restrict blood flow. Also, ask the employee if any items are pressing into his or her flesh.
12.	Return to step 1 and repeat steps 1 through 11 to ensure that the body alignment is still correct in every aspect.			This is done to ensure that subsequent adjustments have not changed the relationship between the individual and the workstation that we achieved during prior adjustments.

Procedure 3.2   *Assessing a Sitting Workstation Without VDT*

Purpose of this procedure

This procedure is designed to determine if there is a mismatch between an employee and a workstation without a VDT and to help you adjust the workstation to prevent the employee from developing musculoskeletal injuries and illness such as back injuries and cumulative trauma disorders. A properly adjusted workstation also helps the employee work at his or her optimal level.

When to use this procedure

Optimally, this procedure should be performed for all employees who work at sitting workstations without VDTs; however, this is not always possible. Therefore, the procedure should be performed if any of the following indicators are observed:

- The employee has experienced a musculoskeletal injury or illness and/or complains about aches and pains at work.

- Several employees in a work unit have experienced musculoskeletal injuries or illnesses while working at similar workstations.

- The employee is observed sitting in an awkward posture:

    The employee's wrists are deviated.

    The employee is leaning forward.

    The employee looks uncomfortable.

    The employee's feet are not supported.

- The employee complains that the workstation is not comfortable.

- The employee's work output is dropping off, and he or she is reporting in sick more often than normal.

- The employee avoids his or her workstation and gravitates toward other employees' offices or conducts work at other locations in the building.

Terms you may not know

Fixture, or jig   A device designed to hold a workpiece in a certain orientation so that work can be performed on it.

Workpiece   Any item an employee is working on—for example, a small engine or a binder to be assembled.

Before you start

Before you perform the procedure, complete the following steps:

1. Familiarize yourself with Figure 3.2A.

2. Make arrangements with the manager and the employee to conduct the assessment.

3. Ensure buy-in from the employee.

4. Obtain a yardstick and a twelve-inch ruler.

5. Obtain a photocopy of Worksheet D.2 in Resource D. This worksheet is a version of the checklist in Exhibit 3.2A.

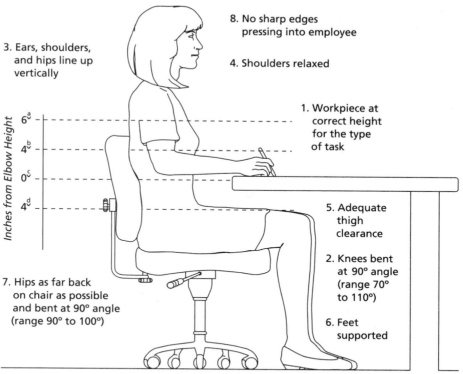

Figure 3.2A. Fundamentals of Good Posture at a Sitting Workstation Without a VDT.

3. Ears, shoulders, and hips line up vertically

8. No sharp edges pressing into employee

4. Shoulders relaxed

1. Workpiece at correct height for the type of task

Inches from Elbow Height

6ᵃ

4ᵇ

0ᶜ

4ᵈ

5. Adequate thigh clearance

2. Knees bent at 90° angle (range 70° to 110°)

7. Hips as far back on chair as possible and bent at 90° angle (range 90° to 100°)

6. Feet supported

Source: Adapted from Ayoub, 1973.

What to do

The goal of this procedure is to adjust the workstation to the employee so he or she can attain a posture like that depicted in Figure 3.2A. The checklist in Exhibit 3.2A will take you through the steps of assessing and adjusting the workstation. Once the employee is adjusted to a proper sitting posture, he or she will be comfortable; so talk to employees about how they feel as you manipulate the various components of their workstations. You may have to perform several iterations of the steps in the checklist before the workstation will be properly adjusted to the employee.

The numbers of the steps in the checklist correspond to the numbers of the descriptions in Figure 3.2A.

Exhibit 3.2A. Checklist for Assessing a Sitting Workstation Without VDT.

Step	Assessment Checklist	Yes	No	How to Do Step
1.	Is the workpiece at the correct height for type of task? • 6 inches above elbow height for fine work like proofing documents or inspecting small parts • 4 inches above elbow height for precision work like mechanical assembly • same height as elbow for writing or light assembly • 4 inches below elbow height for coarse or medium work like packaging If no, adjust the chair height or the height of the workpiece. You can adjust the height of the workpiece by using a document holder for papers or a fixture for mechanical work. Also, you can raise or lower the workbench or desk by adding height to the legs or cutting them shorter.	☐	☐	The piece of work the employee is doing must be at the correct height for the type of work involved. When working on precise tasks, for instance, the piece of work should be brought closer to the eye, to reduce the viewing distance and to provide support for the arms (precise tasks generally are static). Work heights for heavy tasks should be lower than for precise work, to provide room for the tools and materials usually required for heavy tasks and to allow for a wider range of motion for the upper extremities. Ask the employee to sit at the workstation with his or her hands on the workpiece. Measure vertically from the bottom of the elbow joint to the middle of the hands (see Figure 3.2B) to determine if the work is in the correct relationship to the elbow height. It is undesirable for this relationship to be too high or too low. If elevating the work surface is not possible, a padded arm support could be provided.

Step	Assessment Checklist	Yes	No	How to Do Step
				Figure 3.2B. How to Measure Hand Height in Relation to Elbow Height.
				Place a yardstick horizontally at elbow height at the bottom of the elbow joint. The yardstick should be parallel to the floor. Measure from the elbow height to the middle of the hands with another yardstick or a 12-inch ruler.
2.	Are the knees bent at a 90° angle (the angle can range from 70° to 110°)? If no, adjust the chair height or try a different chair.	☐	☐	Eyeball the knee joint and determine if it is bent at a 90° angle.
3.	Are the ears, shoulders, and hips lined up vertically (the head can be tipped slightly forward at a comfortable angle of 5° to 10°)? If no, adjust the chair height, the angle of the backrest, or the viewing distance to the workpiece (see Procedure 5.1).	☐	☐	Step back from the employee and look at the seated posture. You should be able to draw an imaginary straight line pointed down from the ears through the shoulders and hips.
4.	Are the shoulders relaxed? If no, adjust the chair height or the workpiece height.	☐	☐	Ask the employee or just look at him or her to determine whether he or she is scrunching up the shoulders.

Exhibit 3.2A. (Continued)

Step	Assessment Checklist	Yes	No	How to Do Step
5.	Is there adequate thigh and leg clearance? If no, try a desk with a thinner top that provides more leg clearance. Remove the items stored underneath the desk.	☐	☐	The employee needs to be as close to the workpiece as possible. A desk top that is too thick or items stored under the desk can hinder good posture. Ask the employee to sit at the workstation and look to see that there are no obstacles to good posture.
6.	Are the feet supported? If no, the employee needs a footrest because at this point the workstation has been adjusted for the employee's elbow, hips, wrists, and knees.	☐	☐	This is an easy one. Look to see if the feet are flat on the floor.
7.	Is the hip joint bent at approximately a 90° angle (the angle can range from 90° to 100°)? If no, adjust the chair height or try a different chair.	☐	☐	Eyeball the hip joint to determine if it is at a 90° angle.
8.	Are any sharp edges pressing into the employee? If yes, pad the items that are causing problems with light foam rubber or remove them.	☐	☐	Look at the employee sitting at the workstation and determine if the edge of the desk, keyboard, or other items at the workstation are pressing into the employee's flesh. This can constrict blood flow. Also, ask the employee if any items are pressing into his or her flesh.
9.	Return to step 1 and repeat steps 1 through 8 to ensure that the body alignment is still correct in every aspect.			

Example of procedure use

Laura was a computer technician whose job was to assemble advanced PCs for space missions. Laura worked at a sitting workstation, and when her boss, Robert, came by to talk to her, he found her leaning forward as she worked. When Robert asked her why she was sitting in what appeared to be a very uncomfortable posture, Laura said it wasn't bad and that she was doing it because she had some "stuff" stored under her desk. Robert asked if he could look and see what stuff it was, so that he could find another place to store it, if need be. What he found were old PC systems and boxes of paper. He asked Laura why she had kept these items, and she said she felt she might use them some day. Due to Laura's desire to keep the materials, Robert found a better storage area for them. He also explained to Laura that it was important for her to be close to her work in order to minimize the forces on her back, and therefore she should not store materials under her workstation. Robert then performed Procedure 3.2 in order to adjust Laura's desk to her, which resulted in Laura's sitting in a much better posture. Even though Laura had not been complaining of problems, it was important to perform the procedure once her poor posture was observed in order to identify problems before they resulted in injury or illness.

Procedure 3.3 | Selecting a Chair

Purpose of this procedure

A chair that is adjustable and is accepted by the employee is one of the most important factors in ensuring that a sitting workplace is ergonomically correct. A chair that does not fit an employee can lead to back injuries or pain, and an employee who is not able to perform optimally because of his or her discomfort, and/or cumulative trauma disorders (CTDs). This procedure provides you with criteria you can use to decide which chair to purchase. It also helps you to ensure that the employee will accept the chair.

Remember, a chair does not have to be expensive or have all the "bells and whistles" to be good. Its appropriateness is determined by its ability to meet the requirements of the task and the employee. Chairs with the same functionality may vary in cost from $135 to $800. However, price differences may reflect differences in the manner in which the chairs adjust or the length of the warranties.

When to use this procedure

This procedure should be performed whether you are considering buying one chair or many chairs. It should also be performed if you are concerned that a chair is causing an employee any of the following problems:

- The employee's lower legs are falling asleep.
- The employee can not be adjusted to the workplace.
- The employee says, "I hate my chair!" or makes similar complaints.
- The employee sits on anything in his or her office but the chair.

Before you start

The actions you should take before you perform this procedure depend on the number of chairs you are purchasing.

1. If you are purchasing chairs for specific individuals and only they will be using the chairs, make arrangements for the individuals to try out the chairs you will be considering.

2. If you are purchasing numerous chairs and/or many people will be using the same chair, form a chair-buying committee to help you select which chairs to buy.

3. Familiarize yourself with the chair features illustrated in Figure 3.3A.

4. Obtain a photocopy of Worksheet E.1 in Resource E. This worksheet is a version of the checklist in Exhibit 3.3A.

What to do

Chairs come in a wide range of styles, costs, and adjustability, and a large amount of research has been done on what constitutes a "good" chair. The criteria on which this procedure is based come from Grandjean's eight "golden rules" (1987) and the guidance of Rodgers (1983). Remember, however, that a chair may not have to have all the possible kinds of adjustability if only one individual will be using it at a single workstation. But

Figure 3.3A. Chair Criteria.

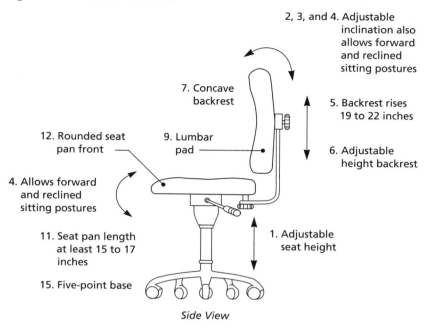

Side View

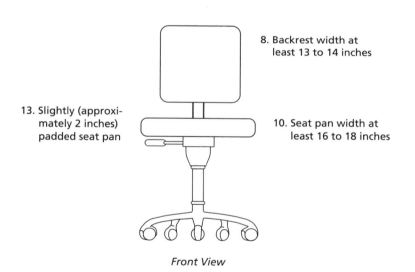

Front View

the chair must allow that individual to sit in a desirable posture while working. The chair also must allow the person to change posture from time to time. The more people who will be using the chair, the more adjustability the chair should have. Keeping these caveats in mind will help you decide what features are more important than others. The checklist in Exhibit 3.3A will ensure that you examine all of a chair's features.

The numbers of the steps in the checklist correspond to the number of the chair features in Figure 3.3A.

Exhibit 3.3A. Checklist for Selecting a Chair.

Step	Selection Checklist	Yes	No	Importance
1.	Does the chair adjust up and down for a seat pan height of between 20 to 26 inches for workstations with footrests and 15.5 to 20 inches for workstations without footrests?	☐	☐	Allows for adjustment to a wide range of work heights.
2.	Does the backrest have an adjustable inclination?	☐	☐	Allows the employee to sit in a wide range of postures.
3.	Does the backrest latch at the desired inclination?	☐	☐	Provides back support in a wide range of postures.
4.	Does the chair allow forward and reclined sitting postures?	☐	☐	Allows the employee to sit in a wide range of postures.
5.	Does the backrest rise 19 to 22 inches vertically above the seat surface?	☐	☐	Provides support for the whole back, thus eliminating pressure on one part of the back.
6.	Is the backrest height adjustable?	☐	☐	Allows adjustability to a wide range of individuals.
7.	Is the upper part of the backrest slightly concave?	☐	☐	Allows the chair to match the natural contour of the back.
8.	Is the width of the backrest at least 13 to 14 inches?	☐	☐	Provides support for the whole back, so there are no pressure points.
9.	Does the backrest have a lumbar pad that provides support to the lumbar spine between the third vertebra and the sacrum, that is, at a height of 4 to 8 inches above the lowest point of the seat surface (this criterion is more important for certain individuals than others)?	☐	☐	Provides support for lumbar region of the back.
10.	Is the seat pan width at least 16 to 18 inches?	☐	☐	Allows the weight of the body to spread over a large area in the sitting posture so there are no pressure points.
11.	Is the seat pan length at least 15 to 17 inches?	☐	☐	Allows the weight of the body to spread over a large area in the sitting posture so there are no pressure points. However, a seat pan that is too long may put pressure on the back of the knee, cutting off the blood supply to the lower leg.

Step	Selection Checklist	Yes	No	Importance
12.	Is the front of the seat pan rounded?	☐	☐	Helps prevent the chair from pressing into the back of the knee and cutting off the blood supply.
13.	Is the seat pan lightly padded (approximately 2 inches thick)?	☐	☐	Helps distribute the weight of the body on the chair.
14.	Does the material covering the chair prevent slipping and draw perspiration away from the body?	☐	☐	Helps prevent the employee from slipping out of the chair and helps prevent heat rash.
15.	Does the chair have a five-point base?	☐	☐	Helps prevent the chair from tipping over.
16.	If the chair has castors, do they lock?	☐	☐	Helps prevent the chair from sliding when the employee does not expect it.
17.	Can the chair be easily cleaned?	☐	☐	If many people are using the chair, it should be easy to clean.
18.	Does the employee feel the chair is acceptable?	☐	☐	An employee might sit in a chair for 8 or more hours a day. Therefore, employees should like their chairs.
19.	Can the employee adjust the chair easily?	☐	☐	This criterion is especially important if more than one employee will be using the chair. Also, be aware that this determination is subjective; what is hard for one employee may be easy for another.
20.	Can the employee make the adjustments without the potential for injury?	☐	☐	Make sure there are no sharp edges that could cut the employee who is adjusting the chair, or parts that could pinch his or her fingers.
21.	How long is the chair's warranty? _____			Helps determine the chair's value.
22.	What is the chair's cost? $_____			Helps determine the chair's value.

Example of procedure use

Kelly, a buyer for a school district, had been tasked with buying chairs for high school students who were taking computer classes. In order to decide which chairs to buy, Kelly obtained a copy of this procedure and Worksheet D.3, and asked several students who represented a wide range of body sizes and shapes if they would like to participate in the chair-buying process. After the students agreed, Kelly arranged to have them visit several potential chair vendors and try out the chairs at computer workstations.

Table 3.3A. Sample Chair Survey Data.

Step Number	Chair 1	Chair 2	Chair 3
1	Y	Y	Y
2	Y	Y	Y
3	Y	Y	Y
4	Y	N	N
5	Y	N	Y
6	Y	Y	Y
7	Y	Y	Y
8	Y	Y	Y
9	N	Y	Y
10	Y	Y	Y
11	Y	N	Y
12	Y	Y	Y
13	N	Y	N
14	Y	Y	Y
15	Y	N	Y
16	Y	Y	Y
17	Y	N	Y
18	Y	N	Y
19	Y	Y	Y
20	Y	Y	Y
21	30 months	12 months	36 months
22	$190	$136	$205

Since the chairs were to be used by a wide variety of persons, they had to be highly adjustable. "Yes" answers to checklist steps 1, 2, 3, 5, 6, and 7 were ranked as very important. For safety and health reasons, yes answers to checklist steps 15, 16, 17, 19, and 20 were also ranked very high. Since the students were not going to be sitting in the chairs for over an hour at one time, yes answers to checklist steps 8, 10, 11, and 12 were ranked lower but still considered important, and the answers to steps 9 and 13 were given low importance. A yes answer to step 18 was ranked moderately high because it is always important to have the user accept the product. The answer to step 21 was used as an indicator of how well the chair was made, because the longer the warranty, the more the manufacturer stands behind the chair's durability. Price, the answer to step 22, was used as the deciding vote. The students visited three chair vendors and collected the data shown in Table 3.3A.

From this information, Kelly chose chair 1 because it had the features that were considered most important, had a good warranty, was accepted by the users, and was the best value for the money.

Procedure 3.4   *Selecting a Sitting Workstation*

Purpose of this procedure

This procedure is designed to help you select an ergonomically sound sitting workstation. Purchasing work desks or tables is expensive, so you must make the right choice for both your employees' health and your budget. When selecting furniture for use by only one individual, you will be less concerned with finding a complete range of adjustability and more concerned with fitting the individual. The more individuals who will be using the furniture, the more adjustability it needs to have.

When to use this procedure

This procedure should be used when you are purchasing new furniture or selecting it from a storage area or other source. You should also perform this procedure when you cannot adjust an employee's current workstation to the employee and you want to find out why you cannot.

Before you start

Before you begin this procedure, complete the following steps:

1. Make arrangements with the employee who will be using the workstation to try out the proposed furniture. Ensure that the employee brings along the chair he or she will be using, because the chair's capabilities have to complement the furniture's capabilities, that is, the furniture's and the chair's ranges of adjustability must match. Otherwise, you may buy a new desk only to find that the chair the employee owns does not allow the employee to be adjusted to the desk.

2. If more than one employee will be using the furniture, form a committee of potential users and make arrangements for the committee to try out all the candidate furniture. This will help ensure that employees buy in to the process and that the furniture will accommodate a wide range of body shapes and sizes.

3. Familiarize yourself with the criteria shown in Figures 3.4A and 3.4B.

4. Obtain a measuring tape or yardstick.

5. Obtain a photocopy of Worksheet E.2 in Resource E. This is a blank version of the checklist in Exhibit 3.4A.

What to do

The procedure in Exhibit 3.4A allows you to determine whether a workstation is right for your employees' needs. Of course, if only one employee will be using the furniture, adjustability is less important than it is when many employees will be using the workstation.

Figure 3.4A illustrates generic criteria for workstations with or without VDTs. Figure 3.4B illustrates additional criteria for sitting workstations with a VDT. The numbers of the criteria in Figures 3.4A and 3.4B correspond to the number of the steps in the checklist in Exhibit 3.4A.

Figure 3.4A. Sitting Workstation Criteria.

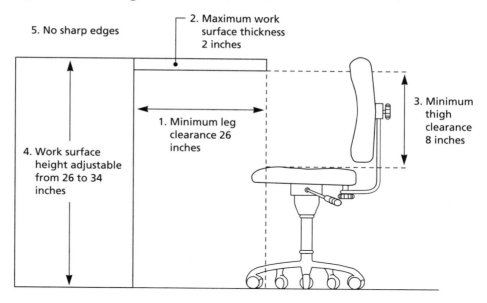

5. No sharp edges

2. Maximum work surface thickness 2 inches

1. Minimum leg clearance 26 inches

3. Minimum thigh clearance 8 inches

4. Work surface height adjustable from 26 to 34 inches

Figure 3.4B. Sitting VDT Workstation Criteria.

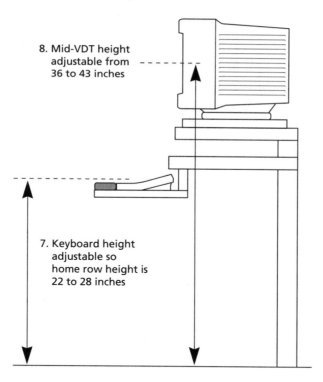

8. Mid-VDT height adjustable from 36 to 43 inches

7. Keyboard height adjustable so home row height is 22 to 28 inches

Exhibit 3.4A. Checklist for Selecting a Sitting Workstation.

Step	Selection Checklist	Yes	No	Importance
1.	Does the workstation provide 26 inches of leg clearance?	☐	☐	Allows the employee to get close to his or her work.
2.	Is the work surface less than 2 inches thick?	☐	☐	Allows the employee to get close to the work without having the workstation bite into the top of the thigh.
3.	Is there approximately 8 inches of thigh clearance?	☐	☐	Allows the employee to get close to the work without having the workstation bite into the top of the thigh.
4.	Is the work surface height adjustable between 26 and 34 inches?	☐	☐	Allows the height to be adjusted to the employee and the task. It is important to ensure that these criteria will meet the needs of the task. Refer to step 1 of Procedure 3.2 to make this judgment. Increase the adjustability if necessary.
5.	Are there sharp edges that could press into the employee?	☐	☐	Smooth edges reduce the potential for the workstation to press into the employee and constrict blood flow.
6.	Is a VDT to be used at this workstation? If no, go to step 9.	☐	☐	
7.	Is the height of the keyboard home row adjustable from 22 to 28 inches?	☐	☐	Allows the keyboard height to be adjusted to a wide range of individuals.
8.	Does the workstation allow the VDT to be used within the viewing distance of the employee at the correct height?	☐	☐	Allows the workstation to accommodate a wide range of individuals. Refer to Procedure 5.1 to determine the correct viewing distance and Procedure 3.1 to determine the correct height for the monitor.
9.	Does the employee accept the workstation?	☐	☐	If the employee does not accept the workstation, he or she may not use it.

Example of procedure use

Using Procedure 3.2, Loreen had tried and failed to adjust a sitting workstation without a VDT to an employee. The employee was of average height and in general fit his workstation well. However, the task was fine inspection, and Loreen and the employee found they could not raise the workpiece high enough for the employee to perform the task well at his current workstation. The company had a large storeroom of old furniture, and Loreen decided to take the employee to the storeroom to find another desk. The employee brought along his chair and a workpiece, and they tried numerous workstations until they found one that met the criteria in Procedure 3.4. It had no sharp edges, it did have enough leg clearance and thigh clearance, and it allowed the workpiece to be examined at the correct height. By discovering that the workstation was wrong for the task and taking the time to select a workstation that met all the criteria for the employee's comfort and ability to perform the task competently, Loreen averted a potential injury and improved the employee's performance.

| Procedure 3.5 | *Assessing a Standing Workstation with VDT* |

Purpose of this procedure

The purpose of this procedure is to determine and correct mismatches between employees and standing workstations where video display terminals (VDTs) are used. Employees have a higher potential for developing cumulative trauma disorders and/or back injuries if mismatches are not detected and corrected. Employees will also not be able to perform at their optimal level if their workstations are not adjusted correctly.

When to use this procedure

This procedure should be performed for every employee who works at a standing workstation and uses a VDT. If this is not possible, perform this procedure when you notice employees in stooped or uncomfortable postures. Assess all workstations where you observe any of the following problems.

- The employee has experienced a musculoskeletal injury or illness and/or complains about aches and pains at work.

- Several employees in a work unit have experienced musculoskeletal injuries or illnesses while working at similar workstations.

- The employee is observed standing in an awkward posture:

    The employee's elbows are not bent at a ninety-degree angle.

    The employee's wrists are deviated.

    The employee is stooped forward.

    The employee looks uncomfortable.

- The employee complains that the workstation is not comfortable.

- The employee's work output is dropping off, and he or she is reporting in sick more often than normal.

- The employee avoids his or her workstation and gravitates toward other employees' offices or conducts work at other locations in the building.

Terms you may not know

Monitor arm A jointed arm-like device on which a computer monitor is placed to give it a great degree of adjustability in every direction.

Normal cone of vision The field within which the eye can easily rotate to see objects.

Wrist rest A device, usually a bar made of firm foam rubber, placed under the wrists to keep them in a neutral posture.

Before you start   Before you perform an ergonomic assessment of a standing workstation with a VDT, complete the following steps:

1. Familiarize yourself with the fundamentals of good posture illustrated in Figure 3.5A.

2. Make arrangements with the manager and the employee to conduct the assessment.

3. Ensure buy-in from the employee.

4. Obtain a yardstick and a twelve-inch ruler.

5. Obtain a photocopy of Worksheet D.3 in Resource D. This worksheet is a version of the checklist in Exhibit 3.5A.

What to do   Use the checklist in Exhibit 3.5 to determine whether an employee is in a desirable standing posture and to adjust the workstation if the employee cannot attain a good posture. There is no one best way of adjusting the workstation because everyone's body dimensions are different. Note that most of the determinations can be made without the aid of any measuring device because they are approximate. Also, once the employee is adjusted to a proper standing posture he or she will feel comfortable, so talk to employees about how they feel as you manipulate the various components of their workstations. You may have to perform several iterations of the steps in the checklist before the workstation will be properly adjusted to the employee.

The numbers of the steps in the checklist correspond to the numbers of the descriptions in Figure 3.5A.

Figure 3.5A. Fundamentals of Good Posture at a Standing Workstation with a VDT.

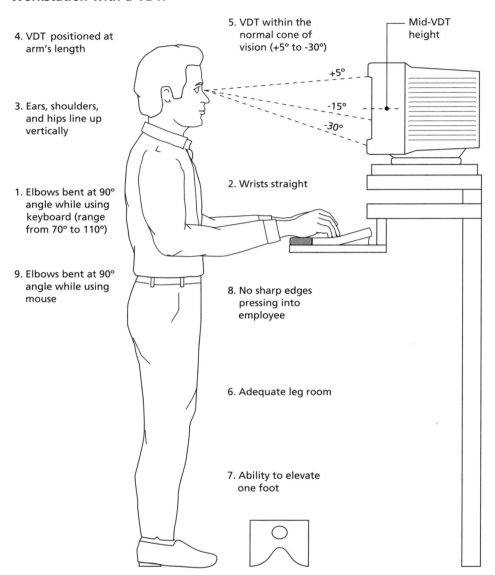

4. VDT positioned at arm's length

3. Ears, shoulders, and hips line up vertically

1. Elbows bent at 90° angle while using keyboard (range from 70° to 110°)

9. Elbows bent at 90° angle while using mouse

5. VDT within the normal cone of vision (+5° to -30°)

Mid-VDT height

+5°
-15°
-30°

2. Wrists straight

8. No sharp edges pressing into employee

6. Adequate leg room

7. Ability to elevate one foot

Source: Adapted from Grandjean, 1987, 1990; American National Standards Institute/Human Factors Society, 1988; and Putz-Anderson, 1988.

Exhibit 3.5A. Checklist for Assessing a Standing Workstation with VDT.

Step	Assessment Checklist	Yes	No	How to Do Step
1.	Is the elbow joint bent at approximately a 90° angle while the employee is using the keyboard and the upper arm is pointing down (the angle can range from 70° to 110°)? If no, adjust the keyboard height. If the keyboard height cannot be adjusted, try a different desk. Most companies have a storage area that is a good source of old furniture. Consider buying a new desk if there is no other way to achieve the correct elbow angle.	☐	☐	Eyeball the employee's elbow joint to determine if it is bent at a 90° angle. You can also hold the corner of a square piece of cardboard up to the joint to compare the 90° angle of the corner to the angle of the elbow.
2.	Are the wrists straight? If no, adjust the height of the keyboard. Try a different desk if the workstation can not be properly adjusted. Also, consider using a wrist rest (see Procedure 4.3).	☐	☐	Look at the wrists to determine if they are straight or deviated. Compare the wrist posture to that in Figure 1.5 in Section One.
3.	Are the ears, shoulders, and hips lined up vertically (the head can be tipped slightly forward at a comfortable angle of 5° to 10°)? If no, adjust the keyboard height or the viewing distance to the VDT (see Procedure 5.1).	☐	☐	Step back from the employee and look at his or her standing posture. You should be able to draw an imaginary straight line pointed down from their ears through their shoulders and hips.
4.	Is the VDT at the proper viewing distance (approximately employee's arm length)? If no, adjust the distance of the monitor from the employee's eyes. Move the monitor forward or back until it is positioned correctly. A monitor arm can help you achieve the correct position.	☐	☐	Ask the employee to stand in his or her optimal posture and reach for the screen. The employee should be able to reach the screen without bending forward and with the back straight. At the same time ask the employee if he or she has any difficulty seeing the screen. You may need to ensure that the lighting levels are correct (see Procedure 5.1).

Exhibit 3.5A. (Continued)

Step	Assessment Checklist	Yes	No	How to Do Step
5.	Is the part of the screen the employee uses most within the normal cone of vision, which is +5° (above the horizontal axis) to −30° (below the horizontal axis)? If no, adjust the height of the VDT by removing the monitor base if the monitor is too high or adding a monitor base on if the monitor is too low. A monitor arm can also be used to raise or lower the VDT.	☐	☐	The mid-VDT height should be about 8 inches below the employee's eye height. You can measure this by holding a yardstick horizontally at the employee's eye level. At the point where the yardstick bisects the monitor, use a shorter ruler to measure 8 inches down.
6.	Is there adequate leg room? If no, remove the obstacles that prevent the employee from attaining a desirable standing posture.	☐	☐	The employee needs to be as close to his or her work as possible. Boxes, materials, and other items the employee "just has to have" that are stored under the workstation can prevent the employee from getting close to the work. Ask the employee to stand at the workstation. Look to see that there are no obstacles to a good posture.
7.	Can the employee elevate one foot? If no, consider installing a rail or finding a small wooden or metal box for this purpose.	☐	☐	A small box or rail on which the employee can elevate one foot at a time reduces fatigue. This box or rail should be 3 to 4 inches tall and about 4 inches wide to be effective.
8.	Are there any sharp edges pressing into the employee? If yes, pad the items that are causing problems with light foam rubber or remove them.	☐	☐	Look at the employee standing at the workstation and determine if the edge of the desk, the keyboard, or other items at the workstation are pressing into the employee's flesh and constricting blood flow. Also, ask the employee if any items are pressing into his or her flesh.

Step	Assessment Checklist	Yes	No	How to Do Step
9.	Is a mouse used at the workstation? If yes, perform steps 9a, 9b, and 9c.	☐	☐	
9a.	Is the elbow bent at a 90° angle (the angle can range from 70° to 110°)? If no, move the mouse closer to the person. An arm support can also be used (see Procedure 4.3).	☐	☐	Eyeball the elbow to determine if it appears to be bent at approximately a 90° angle (see step 1 for an additional method of determining the angle).
9b.	Is the upper arm close to the body? If no, move the mouse closer to the person.	☐	☐	Look to see that the upper arm is close to the body and not abducted (pulled away).
9c.	Is the wrist deviated? If yes, adjust the height of the mouse and/or use a wrist rest (see procedure 4.3).	☐	☐	Look at the wrist to determine whether it is deviated either to the left or right, up or down.
10.	Return to step 1 and repeat steps 1 through 9 to ensure that the body alignment is still correct in every aspect.			

Example of procedure use

Kootenai Designer Trout was a genetic engineering firm that had developed a subspecies of trout that tasted like chicken. Lindsay, a company engineer, walked into the production area one day and saw Samantha, one of the production employees, in a very strange posture. She was stooped over, typing on a keyboard that was on a standard desk while she looked at a display positioned at about her full standing height. Her wrists were also severely deviated. Lindsay asked Samantha why she was in this awful posture, and Samantha explained that the monitor was placed high because the operators only occasionally used the keyboard, but they had to look at the monitor on every shift round. Today, however, she had to change the parameters on a program in the primordial soup that was to become the next wave in designer trout (a trout that tastes like chocolate mousse).

Lindsay next asked Samantha how long the task would take, and she said about three hours. Lindsay told Samantha that if the task would take that long she should be in a standing posture and that he would find something with which to elevate the keyboard. Lindsay left and found an old bench that looked about the right height. After he positioned the keyboard on the bench, Samantha could use the keyboard while standing up straight and with her wrists straight. The monitor was still too high, but its mid-height was within Samantha's line of sight. Lindsay next put in a work order to modify the workstation permanently, so it could be adjusted for all the operators who could be using it.

The new trout Samantha was developing went on to win high honors at the Trout Tasting marathon, and not only did a temporary adjustment prevent a potential injury from occurring immediately, but steps were also taken to prevent injuries to all those who used the workstation over a longer period of time.

Procedure 3.6   *Assessing a Standing Workstation Without VDT*

Purpose of this procedure

The purpose of this procedure is to evaluate a standing workstation without a VDT to determine if there are mismatches between the workstation and the employee. The checklist shows you how to adjust these workstations so that employees can avoid workplace design-related conditions such as back problems, injuries, and cumulative trauma disorders. Employees may also not be working at optimal levels if they are uncomfortable.

When to use this procedure

This procedure should be performed for every employee who works at a standing workstation without a VDT. The following events indicate a need for an ergonomic assessment:

- The employee has experienced a musculoskeletal injury or illness and/or complains about aches and pains at work.

- Several employees in a work unit have experienced musculoskeletal injuries or illnesses while working at similar workstations.

- The employee is observed standing in an awkward posture:

  The employee is stooped forward.

  The employee's wrists are deviated.

  The employee looks uncomfortable.

- The employee complains that the workstation is not comfortable.

- The employee's work output is dropping off, and he or she is reporting in sick more often than normal.

- The employee avoids his or her workstation and gravitates toward other employees' offices or conducts work at other locations in the building.

Terms you may not know

Fixture, or jig   A device designed to hold a workpiece in a certain orientation so that work can be performed on it.

Workpiece   The item the employee is working on—for example, a small engine or a binder to be assembled

Before you start

Before you conduct an ergonomic assessment of a standing workstation, complete the following steps:

1. Familiarize yourself with the fundamentals of good posture in Figure 3.6A.

2. Make arrangements with the manager and the employee to conduct the assessment.

3. Ensure buy-in from the employee.

4. Obtain a yardstick and a twelve-inch ruler.

5. Obtain a photocopy of Worksheet D.4 in Resource D. This worksheet is a version of the checklist in Exhibit 3.6A.

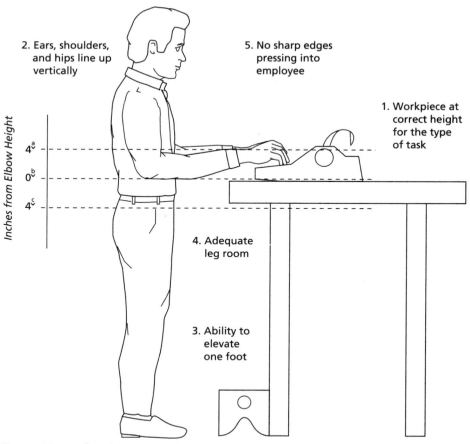

Figure 3.6A. Fundamentals of Good Posture at a Standing Workstation Without a VDT.

2. Ears, shoulders, and hips line up vertically

5. No sharp edges pressing into employee

1. Workpiece at correct height for the type of task

Inches from Elbow Height

4^a

0^b

4^c

4. Adequate leg room

3. Ability to elevate one foot

[a] For precision work with supported elbows
[b] For light assembly work
[c] For heavy work

Source: Adapted from Ayoub, 1977.

What to do

Figure 3.6A shows the fundamentals of good posture at a standing workstation without a VDT. The checklist in Exhibit 3.6A will help you adjust the workstation as the assessment is being conducted until the employee can attain this proper standing posture. There is no one best way of adjusting the workstation because everyone's body dimensions are different. Note that most of the determinations are made without the aid of any measuring device because they are approximate. Also, once the employee is adjusted to a proper standing posture, he or she will feel comfortable, so talk to employees about how they feel as you manipulate the various components of their workstations.

The numbers of the descriptions in Figure 3.6A correspond to the numbers of the steps in the checklist.

Exhibit 3.6A. Checklist for Assessing a Standing Workstation Without VDT.

Step	Assessment Checklist	Yes	No	How to Do Step
1.	Is the workpiece at the correct height for type of task (4 inches above elbow height for precision work with supported elbows, same height as elbow for light assembly work, 4 inches below elbow height for heavy work)? If no, adjust the height of the workpiece by using a document holder for papers or a fixture for mechanical work. Also, you can raise or lower the workbench or desk by adding height to the legs or cutting them shorter.	☐	☐	The piece of work the employee is doing must be at the correct height for the type of work involved. Ask the employee to stand at the workstation with his or her hands on the workpiece. Measure vertically from the bottom of the elbow joint to the middle of the hands (see Figure 3.2B) to determine if the work is in the correct relationship to the elbow height. It is undesirable for this relationship to be too high or too low.
2.	Are the ears, shoulders, and hips lined up vertically (the head can be tipped slightly forward at a comfortable angle of 5° to 10°)? If no, adjust the workpiece height. A physical obstacle, such as items stored under the workstation, may also be hindering the employee from attaining a desirable posture.	☐	☐	Step back from the employee and look at the standing posture. You should be able to draw an imaginary straight line pointed down from the ears through the shoulders and hips.
3.	Can the employee elevate one foot? If no, consider installing a rail or finding a small wooden or metal box for this purpose.	☐	☐	A small box or rail on which the employee can elevate one foot at a time reduces fatigue. This box or rail should be 3 to 4 inches tall and about 4 inches wide to be effective.

Exhibit 3.6A. (Continued)

Step	Assessment Checklist	Yes	No	How to Do Step
4.	Is there adequate leg room? If no, remove the obstacles that prevent the employee from attaining a desirable standing posture.	☐	☐	The employee needs to be as close to his or her work as possible. Boxes, materials, and other items the employee "just has to have" that are stored under the workstation can prevent the employee from getting close to the work. Ask the employee to stand at the workstation. Look to see that there are no obstacles to a good posture.
5.	Are there any sharp edges pressing into the employee? If yes, pad the items that are causing problems with light foam rubber or remove them.	☐	☐	Look at the employee standing at the workstation and determine if the edge of the workstation or other items at the workstation are pressing into the employee's flesh and constricting blood flow. Also, ask the employee if any items are pressing into his or her flesh.
6.	Return to step 1 and repeat steps 1 through 5 to ensure that the body alignment is still correct in every aspect.			

Example of procedure use

Gary was an independent television repair technician who had to work long hours to make a profit. He had been experiencing shoulder pain, however, and this was affecting his productivity. His family physician pre-scribed anti-inflammatory medication and recommended he find someone to do an ergonomic assessment of his workstation. She also recommended that he take more frequent breaks. The ergonomic assessment determined that the workpiece height was eight inches above his elbow height, too high for the weight of the objects Gary was handling, causing his shoulder to become fatigued. To resolve the problem, he built a small platform that was eight inches high and stood on it while he worked at his bench; he also tried to take more breaks. The result of the two corrective actions was greater productivity.

| Procedure 3.7 | *Selecting a Standing Workstation* |

Purpose of this procedure

This procedure is designed to help you select a standing workstation. Purchasing workstations is expensive, so you must make the right choice for both your employees' health and your budget. When selecting furniture for use by only one individual, you will be less concerned with finding a complete range of adjustability and more concerned with fitting the individual. However, the more individuals who will be using the furniture, the more adjustability it needs to have.

When to use this procedure

This procedure should be used when you are purchasing new furniture or selecting it from a storage area or other source. You should also perform this procedure when you cannot adjust an employee's current workstation to the employee and you want to find out why you cannot.

Before you start

Before you begin this complete the following steps:

1. Make arrangements with the employee who will be using the workstation to try out the proposed furniture.

2. If more than one employee will be using the furniture, form a committee of potential users and make arrangements for the committee to try out all the candidate furniture. This will help ensure that employees buy in to the process and that the furniture will accommodate a wide range of body shapes and sizes.

3. Familiarize yourself with the criteria in Figures 3.7A and 3.7B.

4. Obtain a measuring tape or yardstick.

5. Obtain a photocopy of Worksheet E.3 in Resource E. This worksheet is a version of the checklist in Exhibit 3.7A.

What to do

The checklist in Exhibit 3.7A allows you to determine whether a workstation is right for your employees' needs. Of course, if only one employee will be using the furniture, adjustability is less important than it is when many employees will be using the workstation.

Figure 3.7A illustrates generic criteria for workstations with or without VDTs. Figure 3.7B illustrates additional criteria for standing workstations with a VDT. The numbers of the criteria in Figures 3.7A and 3.7B correspond to the numbers of the steps in the checklist.

Figure 3.7A. Standing Workstation Criteria.

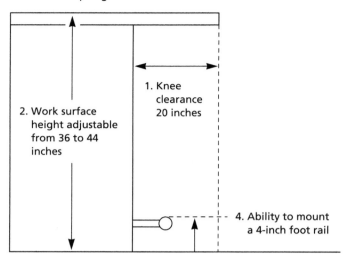

3. No sharp edges

1. Knee clearance 20 inches

2. Work surface height adjustable from 36 to 44 inches

4. Ability to mount a 4-inch foot rail

Figure 3.7B. Standing VDT Workstation Criteria.

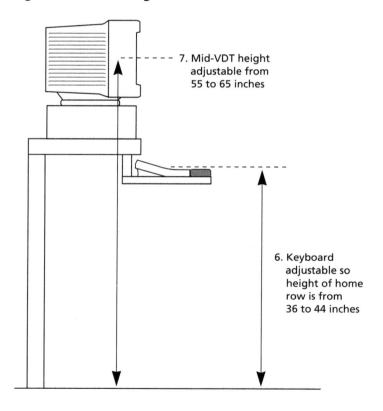

7. Mid-VDT height adjustable from 55 to 65 inches

6. Keyboard adjustable so height of home row is from 36 to 44 inches

Exhibit 3.7A. Checklist for Selecting a Standing Workstation.

Step	Selection Checklist	Yes	No	Importance
1.	Does the workstation provide 20 inches of knee and foot clearance?	☐	☐	Allows the employee to get close to the work.
2.	Is the work surface height adjustable from 36 to 44 inches?	☐	☐	Allows the height to be adjusted to the employee and the task. It is important to ensure that these criteria will meet the needs of the task. Refer to step 1 of Procedure 3.6 to make this judgment. Increase the adjustability if necessary.
3.	Are there sharp edges that could press into the employee?	☐	☐	Smooth edges reduce the potential for the workstation to press into the employee and constrict blood flow.
4.	Does the workstation have a foot rail for elevating one foot?	☐	☐	Reduces leg fatigue.
5.	Is a VDT to be used at this workstation? If no, go to step 8.	☐	☐	
6.	Is the height of the keyboard home row adjustable from 36 to 44 inches?	☐	☐	Allows the keyboard height to be adjusted to a wide range of individuals.
7.	Does the workstation allow a VDT to be used within the employee's viewing distance and at the correct height for the employee?	☐	☐	Allows the workstation the ability to accommodate a wide range of individuals (see Procedure 5.1 to determine the viewing distance and Procedure 3.5 to determine for the correct height for the monitor).
8.	Does the employee accept the workstation?	☐	☐	If the employee does not accept the workstation, he or she may not use it.

Example of procedure use

Snowpack Ice Cream was a new company committed to making ice cream from snow. Their operations were sporadic, however, because it depended on Mother Nature for the raw materials. Jennifer, chief taster of the ice cream, stood all day at a bench that had a work surface height of twenty-nine inches (the standard work surface height of a writing desk), scooping ice cream from cartons and tasting it. When she began to complain about elbow and shoulder aches during one particularly snowy period, Charlie, her manager, applied Procedure 3.6 and determined that the work surface of Jennifer's workbench was too low. Since her task was equivalent to light assembly, Charlie determined that the work surface height should approximate Jennifer's elbow height. He asked Jennifer to stand near the bench in a good posture and measured the height of her elbow from the floor with a five-foot measuring stick. The measurement showed that the work surface should be forty inches, but Jennifer's current bench could not be modified to that height. Charlie hired a carpenter to build a bench that was the correct height, had no sharp edges, and provided adequate knee and foot clearance as described in Procedure 3.7. After Jennifer began using the bench, she had many fewer elbow and shoulder pains.

Work Activities: Eliminating the Risk of Injury

Introduction

This chapter shows you how to identify mismatches between an employee's capacities and the tasks he or she performs. The procedures deal primarily with tasks requiring repetitive hand and wrist motions and with lifting tasks in office settings.

Procedure decision table

The following decision table will help you choose the procedures that will apply to your situation if you have not already completed this step as part of Procedure 2.4.

Procedure	When to Use	Page
4.1. Assessing Workstation Layout	Employee must lean forward to grab objects Employee appears cramped for space	97
4.2. Assessing Tasks Requiring Repetitive Motion of the Upper Extremities	Employee's wrists or shoulders are deviated Employee has upper-extremity musculoskeletal injury Employee performs highly repetitive tasks	103
4.3. Assessing Ergonomic Gadgets	You are preparing to buy an ergonomic gadget such as a wrist rest or arm support	110
4.4. Assessing Tasks Requiring Lifting	Lifting is not a normal part of employee's job Employee has infrequent lifting tasks Office employee has lifting tasks	113

What are the results of the procedures in this chapter?

The procedures in this chapter are designed to improve workplace activities. After you perform these procedures, the workplace and tasks will be modified so that items employees use most often will be within the employees' reach envelopes, the employees' wrists or upper extremities will not be deviated when the employees perform an activity, egresses will be adequately sized and doors will swing in the most appropriate direction, lifting tasks will be better designed, employees will be trained on the causes of cumulative trauma disorders (CTDs) and on how to lift properly, and ergonomic aids will be purchased only if they meet the needs of the task.

For more information

Astrand, P. O., and Rodahl, K. *Textbook of Work Physiology.* New York: McGraw-Hill, 1978.
A book that examines human work physiology and the physiological limitations to performing work.

Ayoub, M. M., and Mital, A. *Manual Materials Handling.* Bristol, Pa.: Taylor and Francis, 1989.
A specific discussion of the ergonomics of manual materials handling and the various models that have been developed for manual materials handling capacities.

Chaffin, D. B., and Andersson, G. B. *Occupational Biomechanics.* New York: Wiley, 1984.
A thorough study of the biomechanical principles of ergonomics and the capacities of humans to perform work in regard to those principles.

Putz-Anderson, V. *Cumulative Trauma Disorders: A Manual for Musculoskeletal Diseases of the Upper Limbs.* Bristol, Pa.: Taylor and Francis, 1988.
The best general book on cumulative trauma disorders.

| Procedure 4.1 | **Assessing Workstation Layout** |

Purpose of this procedure

The purpose of this procedure is to determine if an office or workspace is arranged optimally for the employee: Can the employee move in a natural way while performing an activity? Can the employee perform an activity while staying within his or her optimal reach envelope? Can the employee move from room to room carrying materials without having to pull a door toward himself or herself? Employees can develop cumulative trauma disorders if their workspaces are not arranged properly. For instance, an employee who is forced to work outside his or her optimal reach envelope has a higher potential than other employees for developing thoracic outlet syndrome.

When to use this procedure

This procedure should performed for every employee to ensure that the workstation is arranged for that individual employee. When it is not feasible to assess every workstation, assessments should be conducted under the following circumstances:

- The employee works with his or her arms above shoulder level for long periods.

- The employee is observed continually leaning forward to grasp objects.

- The employee is observed holding large objects while pulling a door toward himself or herself in order to pass through the doorway.

- The employee appears cramped and uncomfortable.

Terms you may not know

Egress An exit.

Life Safety Code A set of standards developed by the National Fire Protection Association (NFPA) to prevent people from being killed due to panic in the event of a fire. The standards deal with such items as door and passageway widths, fire walls, stairways, and so forth. These standards are also OSHA regulations (Lathrop, 1991).

Link analysis An analysis technique that determines physical associations between people and their workplaces.

Before you start

Before you conduct an ergonomic assessment of a workstation layout, complete the following steps:

1. Familiarize yourself with the link analysis technique described in Exhibit 4.1A, the concept of the reach envelope in Figures 4.1A, 4.1B, and 41.C, and the pattern of door swings illustrated in Figure 4.1D and Exhibit 4.1B.

2. Make arrangements with the manager and the employee to conduct the assessment.

3. Ensure buy-in from the employee.

4. Obtain a six-foot measuring tape and a yardstick.

5. Obtain a stopwatch or a watch with a second hand that is easy to read.

6. Obtain a photocopy of Worksheet D.5 in Resource D. This worksheet is a version of the checklist in Exhibit 4.1C.

What to do

Use the checklist in Exhibit 4.1C to assess each workstation's layout and the doorways in the workplace.

Figure 4.1A. Sample Link Analysis and Employee Reach Envelope.

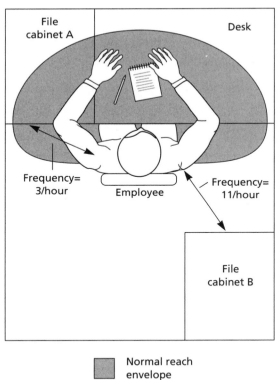

Exhibit 4.1A. Link Analysis.

1. Draw a sketch of the workplace to scale. This can usually be done on an 8½ × 11-inch sheet of paper (see Figure 4.1A).

    a. Draw a circle to represent the employee in his or her normal position.

    b. Represent important pieces of equipment with recognizable symbols, for example, a box for a filing cabinet, a circle for a trash can, and so forth.

    c. Label all parts of the drawing.

2. Ask the employee to perform the job as he or she normally does.

3. Observe the employee performing the job.

4. Draw lines from the employee to the equipment he or she uses. These lines are the links.

5. Note how often the employee uses the equipment per time period.

6. Determine whether the equipment the employee uses most often is within his or her normal reach envelope. The normal reach envelope is shown in Figures 4.1B (side view) and 4.1C (top view).

Figure 4.1B. Side View of Reach Envelope.

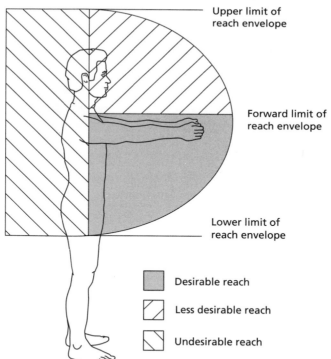

Upper limit of
reach envelope

Forward limit of
reach envelope

Lower limit of
reach envelope

Desirable reach

Less desirable reach

Undesirable reach

Exhibit 4.1B. How to Analyze Door Swing Patterns.

1. Draw a diagram of the building layout showing the doors and rooms of interest (see Figure 4.1D).

2. For a period of time or using work sampling techniques (Barnes, 1980), watch the movement of people and materials in and out of the rooms and through the hallways.

3. Represent these movements with arrows showing the direction of flow. Use a larger or thicker arrow for more flow and a shorter or thinner arrow for less flow.

4. A door should swing bi-directionally if possible, but in the direction of the most flow if only one direction of swing is possible.

5. Doors should always swing in the direction of the flow that would result from an emergency.

Figure 4.1C. Top View of Reach Envelope.

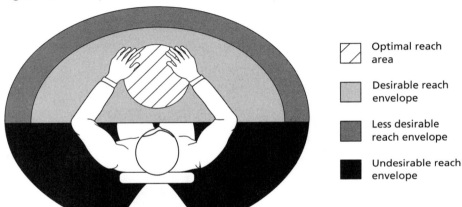

Figure 4.1D. Sample Door Swing Diagram.

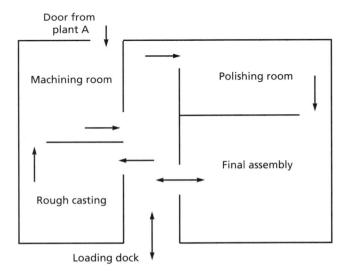

Exhibit 4.1C. Checklist for Assessing Workstation Layout.

Step	Assessment Checklist	Yes	No	How to Do Step
1.	Does the employee have adequate room to attain a full range of motion? If no, rearrange the workplace to allow the employee a full range of motion.	☐	☐	Ask the employee to take his or her normal posture. Then ask the employee to sweep his or her arms in a natural movement. See if there are any obstacles that hinder or obstruct this motion. If the workspace is too confining, the employee may not have the room to stretch and overcome fatigue.
2.	Is the workstation arranged so the objects the employee uses most are closest to him or her and within his or her reach envelope? If no, rearrange the layout so items used are optimally arranged given the employee's reach envelope.	☐	☐	Perform a link analysis to determine this (see Exhibit 4.1A.)
3.	Do the workplace doors swing in the direction of travel? If no, change the direction of the swing of the door or make the door bidirectional. In most cases, this can be done easily with the help of building maintenance personnel.	☐	☐	Figure 4.1D illustrates a door swing diagram and Exhibit 4.1B describes how to analyze door swing patterns. The Life Safety Code (NFPA standard number 101) requires that doors swing in the direction of flow for egress to ensure employees can escape in the event of a fire (Lathrop, 1991). However, employees can injure themselves if they try to carry materials and pull a door open at the same time. Therefore, when possible, doors should swing in the direction of employee movement if the employee will be carrying materials.

Exhibit 4.1C. (Continued)

Step	Assessment Checklist	Yes	No	How to Do Step
4.	Are the doors or openings wide enough? If no, widen the door or opening or institute an administrative control, such as controlling how employees can use the door or opening.	☐	☐	The Life Safety Code (NFPA 101) requires that doors and openings be a certain width. Please consult the latest version of this standard for the minimum requirements. In numerous cases, however, these minimum requirements do not take into account such factors as more than one employee using the door at a time and employees carrying materials. To perform this step, simply observe the employees when they enter or exit the workplace. Note any problems.

Example of procedure use

An employee was observed working for several hours and from these observations the link analysis diagram in Figure 4.1A was developed. This diagram shows that of the fourteen times he accessed the file cabinets in an hour, eleven times he had to go outside his normal reach envelope to obtain files from file cabinet B. Although in a few cases he swiveled his chair to get to the files, in most cases he just reached backward and grabbed the necessary files. When the employee was interviewed, it was determined that there were no reasons why the file cabinets could not be rearranged. So the positions of file cabinet B and file cabinet A were reversed After the file cabinets were moved, the employee could perform most of his necessary motions within his normal reach envelope.

| Procedure 4.2 | **Assessing Tasks Requiring Repetitive Motion of the Upper Extremities** |

Purpose of this procedure

This procedure is performed to determine whether tasks need to be redesigned to minimize employees' potential for developing cumulative trauma disorders (CTDs). CTDs can take a number of years to develop because they are the result of repeated microtraumas to the soft tissues. CTDs have been associated with four risk factors: posture of the body or its parts, repetitive motion, force used to perform the task, and lack of adequate rest to overcome the fatigue of the task. See Table 1.1 for a discussion of the risk factors for specific CTDs. Procedure 4.2 focuses on the upper extremities and the wrists and hands in particular. Consult an ergonomist if the task you are assessing appears to be beyond the scope of this book.

When to use this procedure

This procedure should be performed under the following circumstances:

- Employees perform repetitive tasks using their hands, wrists, arms, or shoulders for long periods of time. Typical repetitive tasks are

    Typing

    Copying

    Using a mouse or track ball

    Using hand tools

    Assembling parts or documents

- Employees experience CTDs or complain of fatigue or aches and pains.

- Employees are observed performing tasks with their wrists, arms, or shoulders in deviated postures.

Terms you may not know

Cumulative trauma disorders A class of musculoskeletal or neurological disorders associated with repetitive tasks that require forceful exertions of the fingers, wrist, hand, elbow, or shoulder.

Fixture, or jig Device that holds an object in a desired configuration.

Microbreaks Short breaks taken relatively frequently to overcome fatigue.

Palmar Flexion A wrist position in which the hand is flexed toward the palm.

Radial deviation Deviation of the wrist toward the radius, a bone on the same side of the forearms as the thumb (see Figure 1.6).

Static work Work that requires the employee to hold stressful posture for a period of time. There is no exact period of time that the posture must be held in order to be called static. The determination is dependent on the muscles being used and the posture.

Ulnar deviation Deviation of the wrist toward the ulna, a bone on the same side of the forearm as the little finger (see Figure 1.6).

Before you start

Before conducting an ergonomic assessment to determine if employees perform repetitive motions of the upper extremities, complete the following steps:

1. Familiarize yourself with the neutral and deviated (good and bad) postures illustrated in Figures 4.2A, 4.2B, 4.2C, and 4.2D.
2. Make arrangements with the manager and the employee to conduct the assessments.
3. Ensure buy-in from the employee.
4. Obtain a stopwatch or a watch with a second hand that is easy to read.
5. Obtain a photocopy of Worksheet D.6 in Resource D. This worksheet is a version of the checklist in Exhibit 4.2A.

What to do

When investigating a task for possible ergonomic problems, your primary objective is to look for the four risk factors associated with CTDs: repetition, the force required by the task, deviated wrist and upper extremity postures, and lack of adequate rest to overcome fatigue (Putz-Anderson, 1988). The risk factors most easily controlled are the amount of rest and the number of repetitions of the task. Next most easily controlled is the posture required by the task. The amount of force an employee uses to perform a task is difficult to control. Therefore, controlling force is not discussed in this procedure.

Example of procedure use

As Tom, an assembly-line supervisor, made his early morning walk-around, he noticed that Buffy's wrists were severely deviated while she performed a series of assembly steps. Knowing that the wrists should not be deviated while performing tasks, Tom reviewed Procedures 2.3 (employee interviews), 3.2 (the assessment of a sitting workstation without a VDT), and 4.2 (assessment of tasks involving repetitive motion of the upper extremities), and made copies of the corresponding worksheets, in order to determine whether the task was contributing to Buffy's potential for developing CTD.

He informed Buffy that he would do an ergonomic assessment, and he interviewed her about the task. The interview revealed that Buffy did experience fatigue in her hands and forearms at the end of the day. Tom then applied Procedure 3.2 and found that the workstation was properly adjusted for Buffy, but when he performed step 1 of Procedure 4.2, he found that Buffy did perform the task with her wrists deviated. From these procedures, Tom knew he needed to modify the task so that Buffy could perform it with her wrists in more neutral postures. For one thing, it appeared that the tools Buffy used contributed to the deviation of her wrists.

Tom next performed step 2. Since he could not see all the separate motions clearly enough to count them, he asked Buffy to perform the assembly slowly, and he determined that the assembly required the following motions: three ulnar wrist deviations, one radial wrist deviation, and two pal-

Figure 4.2A. Shoulder Postures.

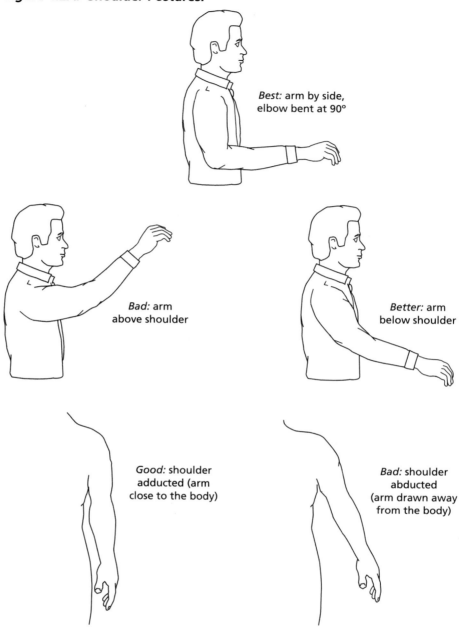

Best: arm by side, elbow bent at 90°

Bad: arm above shoulder

Better: arm below shoulder

Good: shoulder adducted (arm close to the body)

Bad: shoulder abducted (arm drawn away from the body)

mar flexions. Buffy produced 350 subassemblies per hour. Therefore, the number of wrist motions performed per hour were

3 ulnar wrist deviations × 350 subassemblies = 1050 ulnar deviations

1 radial deviation × 350 subassemblies = 350 radial deviations

2 palmar flexions × 350 subassemblies = 700 palmar flexions

Clearly, the task was highly repetitive. The answer to step 3 was no. Tom did not feel Buffy had enough break time, and he knew she had not been trained on what caused CTDs so the answer to step 4 was also no.

Figure 4.2B. **Tool Design and Wrist Postures.**

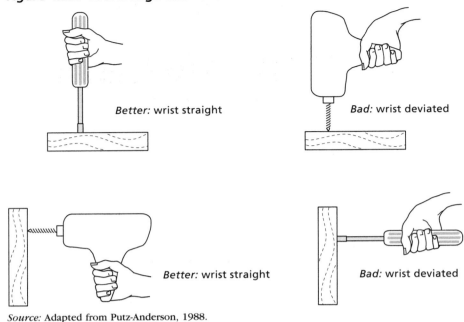

Better: wrist straight

Bad: wrist deviated

Better: wrist straight

Bad: wrist deviated

Source: Adapted from Putz-Anderson, 1988.

Figure 4.2C. **Common Grip Postures.**

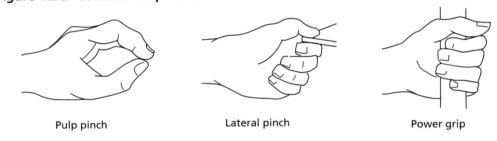

Pulp pinch

Lateral pinch

Power grip

Figure 4.2D. **Elbow and Forearm Rotations, Viewed from the Position of the Fist.**

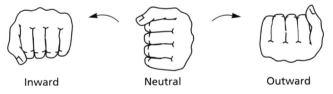

Inward

Neutral

Outward

To improve the task, Tom found new tools that were curved and allowed Buffy to keep her wrists in a more neutral posture. He also decided to rotate Buffy with Robert, who performed a task that required different body motions, every hour in order to reduce the number of repetitions of both employees. Tom also had an industrial hygienist conduct meetings with the entire staff about the risk factors associated with CTDs and the concept of microbreaks.

Exhibit 4.2A. Checklist for Assessing Tasks Requiring Repetitive Motion of the Upper Extremities.

Step	Assessment Checklist	Yes	No
1.	Is the employee observed performing a task with the wrist or an upper extremity deviated?	☐	☐

If yes, modify the task using any of the following methods:

- Change the tool used to perform the task. Figure 4.2B shows how a different tool can change wrist postures. The ergonomic design philosophy is *bend the tool, not the human.* (Emanuel, Mills, and Bennett, 1980)

- Adjust the workstation (see the procedures in Chapter Three).

- Use wrist rest to keep the wrist in a neutral posture for typing tasks (see Procedure 4.3).

- Use a jig or fixture to position the workpiece comfortably rather than allow the employee to deviate his or her posture to work on the item.

How to Do Step

Figure 4.2E shows the wrist in neutral and deviated postures. The wrist does not need to be in a neutral posture all the time; however, the more time the wrist is used in a neutral posture the less potential there is for problems to develop, the more deviated the wrist the higher the potential for problems. Figure 4.2A shows deviated, or bad, shoulder postures. Also, you should consider overhead work with the arms as undesirable

Figure 4.2E. Wrist Postures.

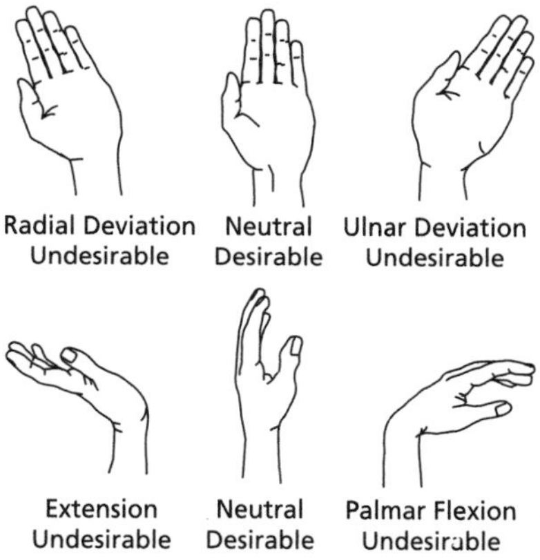

Radial Deviation Undesirable · Neutral Desirable · Ulnar Deviation Undesirable

Extension Undesirable · Neutral Desirable · Palmar Flexion Undesirable

Exhibit 4.2A. (Continued)

Step	Assessment Checklist	Yes	No	How to Do Step
2.	Is the task highly repetitive? If yes, reduce the number of repetitions by automating the task or by alternating the tasks the employee performs. For example, have employee A perform task A for a 2-hour period and then alternate tasks with employee B who is performing task B. This only works, however, if the sets of motions required by tasks A and B are different. Or develop a matrix of tasks and their demands and schedule the tasks so that the employee does not perform like tasks sequentially. (The cycle time of the task and the percentage of the time the employee performs similar motions within that cycle are also important indicators of a stressful task. However, determining cycle times is difficult and an ergonomic expert should be consulted.)	☐	☐	There is no absolute figure for a bad number of repetitions per hour; however, 1,200 to 1,500 repetitions per hour seems to be generally agreed upon as a bad number of repetitions, especially if the employee is performing the motions in a deviated posture. Observe the task for short periods and count repetitions for 5 to 10 minutes at a time. From these observations, you can estimate how many times the task is performed per hour. A second technique is to ask the employee to perform the task very slowly. Count the number of motions and multiply this number by the total number of parts the employee produces per hour. Include in the count the number of grips as shown in Figure 4.2C and elbow rotations as shown in Figure 4.2D.
3.	Is the employee who performs repetitive tasks or static work provided with enough rest breaks? If no, the employee should be encouraged to take a microbreak every 30 minutes and to perform stretching exercises during that break. Microbreaks have no absolute minimum or maximum timespan; however, they should last from 30 seconds to 1 minute. A physical therapist should be consulted to develop a stretching program. Memory resident computer programs can be set up to remind employees to take short breaks at preset intervals.	☐	☐	The standard 15-minute rest break every 2 hours may not be adequate to overcome the fatigue associated with repetitive tasks. Alternatively, the 15-minute break may be enough time but may not be provided when the rest is needed. A better method is to provide short breaks every hour and to encourage the employee to take microbreaks.

Step	Assessment Checklist	Yes	No	How to Do Step
4.	Has the employee been trained on the risk factors associated with CTDs?	☐	☐	All employees should learn what causes CTDs. When they are aware of the risk factors, employees will know what postures to avoid and when to inform management that a task needs redesign.

4. Has the employee been trained on the risk factors associated with CTDs? ☐ ☐

If no, train the employee. It is beyond the scope of this book to present all the information needed in a CTD training program; however, a desirable program covers the following areas:

- Previous CTDs in the company and the department
- The four risk factors associated with CTDs: deviated postures, numerous repetitions, lack of adequate rest to overcome fatigue, and use of force in deviated postures
- The need to report ergonomic problems to management

This training should be provided upon employment and annually thereafter.

All employees should learn what causes CTDs. When they are aware of the risk factors, employees will know what postures to avoid and when to inform management that a task needs redesign.

Procedure 4.3 — Assessing Ergonomic Gadgets

Purpose of this procedure

This procedure is designed to help you decide whether a wrist rest or arm support will help an employee. Such ergonomic gadgets are somewhat controversial and the National Institute for Occupational Safety and Health (NIOSH) and Occupational Safety and Health Administration (OSHA) have not decided on the effectiveness of the devices on the market. Therefore, keep abreast of the latest information to ensure that you are complying with the law. Also, do not buy anything before you check it out. Buying a certain wrist rest for all your employees and later finding out that no one or only a few people like it could be an expensive mistake.

This procedure does not address back belts and wrist splints. I feel that the use of these devices requires the oversight of a physician to ensure that the device does not contribute to a physical problem. Glare screens are addressed in Procedure 5.2.

When to use this procedure

This procedure should be conducted whenever you are considering an ergonomic gadget for use.

Terms you may not know

Arm support A device that typically attaches to the workstation or desk in order to support the forearm. There are many styles of arm supports available (see Figure 4.3A).

Figure 4.3A. Arm Support.

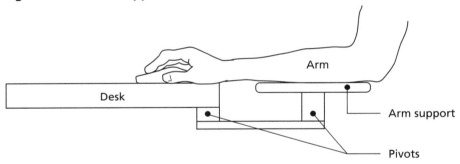

Wrist rest A device, usually made of firm foam rubber, that is used to keep the wrists in a neutral posture.

Before you start

Before you perform this procedure, you should complete the following steps:

1. Perform the procedures in Chapter Three to ensure that the workstation is properly adjusted. An ergonomic gadget is not the solution to a workplace that is not properly adjusted.

2. Obtain samples of the gadget from the vendor.

3. Ask the vendor for a list of references whom you can call to find out whether other companies like the gadget.

4. Consult the latest information from NIOSH and OSHA to ensure that you are complying with the law and current government guidelines.

5. If the gadget is a wrist rest, familiarize yourself with Exhibit 4.3A and Figure 4.3B.

You do not need a worksheet to perform this brief procedure.

Exhibit 4.3A. Proper Wrist Rest Usage.

The purpose of wrist rests is to keep the wrists in a neutral posture when typing. Wrist rests are effective for those individuals who can be described as lazy typists, that is, they rest the palm of the hand on the typing desk while typing. This can cause the wrist to be extended, putting stress on the wrist. Wrist rests are probably not as effective for wrist postures in which the wrist is flexed. In these cases, the typist's chair probably needs to be lowered until the wrist is in a more neutral posture.

Figure 4.3B shows both good and bad examples of wrist rest usage. A good indicator of whether it is being used correctly and effectively is to ask the employee if, after a trial period of at least one to two weeks, he or she experiences less wrist fatigue with or without a wrist rest. If after that time the person experiences more fatigue with the rest than without it, discard it.

Wrist rests that are metal or hard plastic and not covered with approximately one-quarter inch of foam rubber should be avoided. Wrists rests that are not fairly firm should be avoided.

Figure 4.3B. Proper Wrist Rest Usage.

Good: Wrist rest helps keep wrist in neutral posture

Bad: no wrist rest and sharp pressure point

Bad: no wrist rest and wrist deviated

Wrist rest

Bad: wrist rest causes wrist deviation

Exhibit 4.3B. Checklist for Assessing Ergonomic Gadgets.

Step	Assessment Checklist	Yes	No	How to Do Step
1.	Does the gadget perform its intended function? If no, discard gadget. Typically, the employee will know whether it is helping or not. If the employee complains that the gadget is causing any problems, such as pain, discomfort, or additional fatigue, then stop its use immediately.	☐	☐	Give the gadget to several employees and let them try it for at least a week because for the first one to two days any gadget, good or bad, will feel unfamiliar to the employees. Watch them use the gadget. Then, through interviews and direct observation, determine if the gadget does what it is supposed to do. (Figure 4.3A and Exhibit 4.3A present information on the use of wrist rests.)
2.	Is there a choice of gadgets available for the employee? If no, consider trying several gadgets for use by the company.	☐	☐	What works for one employee may not work for another. So have a selection of gadgets instead of one standard gadget.

What to do

The steps in this procedure allow you to determine whether the gadget is effective for use and performs its intended function. The device must not force the body into a bad posture or cause the employee pain, discomfort, or fatigue. If it does, stop using it immediately.

Example of procedure use

Jiffee Typing Term Papers had twenty typists and five of them used wrist rests but fifteen did not. The ones who used wrist rests had bought them at various computer stores or through catalogs. Mary Jiffee wanted to determine whether the wrist rests were effective, because, if they were, she wanted to buy them for all her employees. Since there were already five models in use and all the workstations had been properly adjusted using Procedure 3.2, she decided to interview the employees using the wrist rests and to watch those employees to see if the rests kept their wrists in neutral postures. Wrist rests A, B, and E appeared to be performing their function. Wrist rests C and D did not. In fact, gadget C was causing the employee pain. Mary asked that employee to stop using the device immediately. Next Mary obtained one more each of wrist rests A, B, and E and allowed each employee to try all of them. After the employees had tried the rests, it turned out that each rest was preferred by some of the employees. Also, seven of the employees did not like any of the wrist rests and said these gadgets interfered with their ability to type. Mary asked all the employees to ask her from now on before they brought in ergonomic gadgets so that she could evaluate the gadgets before employee use.

| Procedure 4.4 | **Assessing Tasks Requiring Lifting** |

Purpose of this procedure

This procedure is performed to determine whether employees are exposed to risk factors associated with back injuries when performing lifting tasks. This particular procedure should be considered only a screening procedure. Manual materials handling (lifting) is a complex activity and an ergonomist should be contacted to assess frequent lifting tasks.

When to use this procedure

This procedure is designed to be used for employees who perform lifting tasks occasionally in their jobs, including

- Lifting less than a few boxes per day
- A lifting task not written into employees' job descriptions
- Repetitive lifting in which no more than two containers are lifted per hour

Consult an ergonomist if the task you are assessing appears beyond the scope of this book. Employees who have complained of back pain or had previous back injuries should have their lifting tasks evaluated first.

Before you start

Before conducting an ergonomic assessment to determine if lifting tasks are being done properly complete the following steps:

1. Familiarize yourself with Exhibit 4.4A and Figure 4.4A, which illustrate lifting limits you will need to know.
2. Make arrangements with the manager and the employee to conduct the assessment.
3. Ensure buy-in from the employee.
4. Obtain a six-foot measuring tape and a yardstick.
5. Obtain a scale. A bathroom scale works well; however, a mailroom scale used for weighing boxes works better.
6. Obtain a photocopy of Worksheet D.7 in Resource D. This worksheet is a version of the checklist in Exhibit 4.4B.

What to do

Most of the loads that employees lift in offices, or in other work settings where lifting is not a standard part of employees' jobs, are boxes of paper or other items contained in boxes of standard dimensions. Most employees who lift boxes or other items in these settings do so because they want to avoid the hassle of finding the maintenance people and asking them to perform the lifting task. Therefore, the employees lift the boxes themselves and wind up hurting their backs because they lifted too much weight, did not lift correctly, were not anticipating the lift, or did not use the proper piece of mechanical equipment because it was unavailable. This procedure is designed to assess these risk factors.

Exhibit 4.4A. Lifting Limits.

Range (0 = Floor Level)	Limit
0 to 29 inches	44 pounds
0 to 65 inches	41 pounds
29 to 65 inches	33 pounds

These limits are based on the following assumptions:

- One lift per minute (assuming only two containers per hour).
- A 12-inch-wide × 17-inch-deep × 12-inch-high box. This is the standard box that computer paper comes in.
- The limits will accommodate both males and females.
- The employee lifts less than one hour per day.

Figure 4.4A. Assessing Lifting Tasks and Lifting Posture.

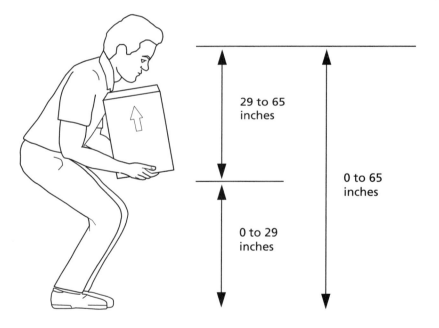

29 to 65 inches

0 to 65 inches

0 to 29 inches

Exhibit 4.4B. Checklist for Assessing Tasks Requiring Lifting.

Step	Assessment Checklist	Yes	No	How to Do Step
1.	Weigh the container the employee is lifting: _____ pounds			There is no hard limit for maximum loads for lifting. However, the values listed in Exhibit 4.4A are limits for lifting for three ranges, floor to 65 inches (top of a medium-high shelf), floor to 29 inches (standard table height), and 29 inches to 65 inches. These limits were calculated using the NIOSH lifting equation (National Institute for Occupational Safety and Health, 1981).
2.	Determine the approximate lift range (see Exhibit 4.4A and Figure 4.4A). Use your judgment and choose the closest match. 0 to 29 inches ☐ ☐ 29 to 65 inches ☐ ☐ 0 to 65 inches ☐ ☐			
3.	Compare the weight of the container to the weight limit for that range (see Exhibit 4.4A). Weight limit: _____ pounds.			
4.	Is the employee lifting more than he or she should? If yes, then mechanical means should be used or the weight of the container should be reduced. Most likely, the mechanical means would be a hand truck or cart that is staged close to its point of use. Employees will use such equipment if it is readily available. (Simply forbidding office workers from performing such tasks does not work because the employees will continue to find it easier to lift boxes themselves and face the consequences than to take the time to locate the person who is supposed to do such lifting.)	☐	☐	

Exhibit 4.4B. (Continued)

Step	Assessment Checklist	Yes	No	How to Do Step
5.	Has the employee been trained about the hazards of improper lifting?	☐	☐	All employees should be given training concerning the hazards of improper lifting.

5. Has the employee been trained about the hazards of improper lifting?

If no, train the employee. The rules for lifting should be included in a training program. Employees shall also be informed about any lifting tasks that have resulted in employee injuries. The rules of lifting are as follows:

- Anticipate the load: that is, predetermine if the load is heavy or light. This can be done by gently moving the box with your foot.

- Evaluate the lifting path: that is, determine if there are obstacles in the way. Make sure there is a place to put the container at the top of the lift.

- Keep the back straight and bend the knees to grasp the load. Figure 4.4A on page 114 demonstrates this posture.

- Use the handles on the container if any are provided.

- Lift with a smooth motion. Don't jerk.

- Keep the load as close to the body as possible when lifting.

- Ensure that the floor is dry and clean so your feet do not slip.

Example of procedure use

Samantha, a human performance technologist who worked in the training department of a large chemical company, was charged with developing training and providing it to the various production plants around the country. One day she noticed Lindsay lifting an apparently heavy box from the floor to the top of a table. He appeared to be struggling with the box, and he was lifting in a stooped posture.

After Lindsay was done with the lift Samantha asked him if the box was heavy. Lindsay replied with a resounding yes. Samantha told him that lifting things that were too heavy could injury a person's back, and she asked Lindsay if he would agree to her assessing this task. After Lindsay agreed, Samantha performed Procedure 4.4.

Using a bathroom scale, she found that the container weighed eighty-two pounds. Then she measured the height of the table with a yardstick to establish the range of the lift, which was zero to twenty-nine inches. The recommended weight for this lift was forty-four pounds or less, so the weight of the container exceeded the recommended limit. Samantha next asked what was in the container, and Lindsay said it was binders of training materials. Samantha asked if they could be put into two containers, and Lindsay said there would be no problem with doing that since they were just being shipped to a plant for a training session. Finally, Samantha explained to Lindsay how he should lift and described the risk factors for back injuries. Lindsay agreed to use good lifting habits in the future.

This example shows how the procedure can be performed in order to assess a task independently of others performing other procedures. This should be done, however, only if the task being assessed can be isolated from the rest of the work environment or activities.

Environment: Ensuring Proper Lighting and Visibility

Introduction

This chapter addresses environmental factors that can contribute to physical problems in the workplace and that you can change. This book cannot address the thermal environment, noise, and vibration because they typically represent complex problems and because governmental regulations are often involved in problem solutions. Please consult an ergonomist or industrial hygienist if you feel you have a problem with heat or cold, noise, or vibration. Smith and Kearny (1994) discuss these factors in relation to their effect on the ability to perform mental work.

Procedure decision table

Use the following table to select the procedures in this chapter that you should perform, unless you have already completed this step as part of Procedure 2.4.

Procedure	When to Use	Page
5.1. Assessing Lighting and Viewing Distance	Lighting is poor Lighting is uneven Viewing distance may be inappropriate for employee	121
5.2. Eliminating Glare from VDTs	Employee has glare on VDT	126

What are the results of the procedures in this chapter?

Employees rely on their vision for most of the tasks they perform; therefore lighting is very important for the performance of most tasks. If employees cannot see clearly what they are working on, it is difficult for them to do the task correctly, and they may develop such physical problems as eye-strain. After you perform Procedure 5.1, your employees should have ample light to see what they need to do to perform the task well. If there were lighting problems before you performed procedure 5.1, you should see an improvement in product quality after the adjustments have been made.

Glare on video display terminals (VDTs) is both an annoying and, to a certain degree, a physically detrimental problem. The result of eliminating glare on a monitor will be an improvement in the employee's ability to perform work. Eliminating glare should also reduce the amount of time needed to do the work.

For more information

American Optometric Association.
   A good source of information on lighting and viewing distance. They publish brochures on the subject, and some of the brochures are free. Their address is American Optometric Association, 243 N. Lindbergh Blvd., St. Louis, MO 63141.
Grandjean, E. *Ergonomics in Computerized Offices.* Bristol, Pa.: Taylor and Francis, 1987.
   An excellent book on office ergonomics, although the information is presented from an ergonomist's point of view. Includes information on lighting and glare.
Rodgers, S. H. *Ergonomic Design for People at Work.* Belmont, Calif.: Lifetime Learning Publications, 1983.
   A Kodak publication that has very good information about workplace design from an industrial point of view.
Smith, P., and Kearny, L. *Creating Workplaces Where People Can Think.* San Francisco: Jossey-Bass, 1994.
   Along with this book, one of the first three volumes in the NSPI series From Training to Performance in the Twenty-First Century.

| Procedure 5.1 | Assessing Lighting and Viewing Distance |

Purpose of this procedure

The purpose of this procedure is to ensure that workplace lighting and viewing distance are adequate for each task. Lighting that is too low and/or a viewing distance that is inappropriate for a particular task can cause such physical problems as sore or burning eyes, eyestrain, and neck tension. These ergonomic problems can also cause product quality problems.

When to use this procedure

Ideally, this procedure should be performed for every workplace; however, assessing every workplace is not always economically practical. Therefore, use these indicators to help you decide whether to perform the procedure for an employee:

- The employee complains of poor light.
- The employee experiences eyestrain or burning eyes, or complains of blurred vision.
- The employee leans toward the work in order to see it better.
- The employee brings in lights from home to use at his or her workstation.
- The employee is not performing an inspection task to the standard required.

Terms you may not know

Document stand A device that holds a document to be read.
Footcandle A U.S. measure of illumination. One footcandle equals approximately ten lux.
Illumination Amount of light falling on a surface.
Lux An SI (International System of Units, or metric) measure of illumination.
Task lighting Lighting provided close to the point of work.
Viewing distance Distance from the eye to the object being viewed.

Before you start

Before conducting an ergonomic assessment to determine if the workstation is properly lighted and arranged for viewing, complete these steps:

1. Familiarize yourself with the information about light meter usage (Figure 5.1A) and about lighting requirements for various tasks (Table 5.1A) and viewing distances for various tasks (Table 5.1B).
2. Make arrangements with the manager and the employee to conduct the assessment.
3. Ensure buy-in from the employee.
4. Obtain a six-foot measuring tape or a yardstick.
5. Obtain a light meter.
6. Obtain a photocopy of Worksheet D.8 in Resource D. This worksheet is a version of the checklist in Exhibit 5.1A.

Table 5.1A. Industrial Lighting Requirements.

Area or Task	Range of Illumination	
	Lux	Footcandles
Public areas with dark surroundings	20–50	2–5
Simple orientation for short temporary visits	50–100	5–9
Working spaces where visual tasks are only occasionally performed; warehouse operations	100–200	9–19
Visual tasks involving high-contrast or large-sized items: reading printed material for typed originals; performing rough bench and machine work or ordinary inspection	200–500	19–46
Computer usage	200–500	19–46
Visual tasks involving medium-contrast or small-sized items: reading penciled handwriting or poorly printed or reproduced material; performing medium bench and machine work, difficult inspection, or medium assembly	500–1,000	46–93
Visual tasks involving low-contrast or very small-sized items: reading handwriting in hard pencil on poor-quality paper or very poorly reproduced material; performing very difficult inspection	1,000–2,000	93–186
Visual tasks involving low-contrast or very small-sized items over a prolonged period: performing fine assembly, highly difficult inspection, or fine bench and machine work	2,000–5,000	186–464
Very prolonged and exacting visual tasks: performing the most difficult inspection, extra-fine bench and machine work, or extra-fine assembly	5,000–10,000	464–929

Table 5.1A. (Continued)

Area or Task	Range of Illumination	
	Lux	Footcandles
Very special visual tasks of extremely low contrast and small size: performing some surgical procedures	10,000–20,000	929–1858

Source: Adapted from Rodgers 1983, and the American Optometric Association, 1992, p. 259.

Table 5.1B. Viewing Distance Requirements.

Task Type	Viewing Distance
Especially visually demanding: performing assembly work or inspection	5 to 10 inches
Visually demanding: performing sewing or drawing	10 to 14 inches
Normal: performing reading or milling	14 to 20 inches
Visually undemanding: packing boxes or performing janitorial work	>20 inches

Source: Adapted from Finnish Institute of Occupational Health, 1989.

What to do

Use the checklist in Exhibit 5.1A to determine whether the lighting levels and the viewing distance for a task are correct. If you have observed possible problems, assess those workstations first.

Example of procedure use

Cheryl and Henry were service managers in a car dealership. To ensure that the mechanics had enough light, Cheryl and Henry conducted lighting surveys of all the service bays, taking light readings where the mechanics actually performed the work—under car hoods, in wheel wells, and in similar places.

The light readings they recorded were in the 30 to 40 footcandle range. Cheryl and Henry determined that car repair tasks should be considered medium assembly, which requires 46 to 93 footcandles of illumination. To increase the lighting level, Henry and Cheryl provided task lighting in the form of portable lights that the mechanics could use to direct light exactly where they needed it.

Exhibit 5.1A. Checklist for Assessing Lighting and Viewing Distance.

Step	Assessment Checklist	Yes	No	How to Do Step
1.	What is the current lighting level: __ footcandles __ lux			Use a light meter as shown in Figure 5.1A to measure lighting levels. **Figure 5.1A. Light Meter Usage.** Employee's field of view / Light meter 1. To measure the lighting level, place a light meter in the employee's field of view. Each light meter is different, so follow the instructions for use that come with yours. Usually the lighting level is read directly from the light meter. It will be in either lux (SI units) or footcandles (U.S. standard units). 2. Compare the light meter reading with the level listed for a similar task in Table 5.1A. If the lighting level is too low, additional lighting is indicated.
2.	What is the lighting level requirement for the task (see Table 5.1A): __ footcandles __ lux			
3.	Compare the values found in steps 1 and 2. Are the lighting levels correct for the task? If no, supply more light to the task. Task lighting (placing a light source where it will shine directly on the task) can be used to correct minor lighting problems. However, major lighting problems may require a building modification and expert assistance.	☐	☐	Excessive amounts of light can weaken information cues and, therefore, decrease ability to perform the task (McCormick and Sanders, 1982). For most tasks, the amount of light provided should not exceed the maximum of the range for workplaces where VDTs are used shown in Table 5.1A.

Step	Assessment Checklist	Yes	No	How to Do Step
				Figure 5.1B. An Example of Task Lighting.
				Illuminated area from overhead fixture
				Employee
4.	What is the viewing distance: ___ inches			With a yardstick or tape measure, check the viewing distance by measuring the distance from the employee's eye to the object being viewed when the employee is in an optimal posture at the workstation.
5.	What is the viewing distance requirement for this task (see Table 5.1B): ___ inches.			
6.	Compare the distances found in steps 4 and 5. Is the viewing distance correct for the task? If no, adjust the viewing distance. There are numerous ways of doing this; for example: • Adjust the workstation (see the procedures in Chapter Three). • Place the work on a stand, such as a document stand, or on a fixture or jig.	☐	☐	The viewing distances shown in Table 5.1B might not accommodate all workers because of individual variations in how the eyes focus. The eyes of nearsighted individuals do not accommodate (focus) the same as the eyes of farsighted individuals. Therefore, take care to ensure when setting up a visual task that the viewing distance for each individual worker is not too long or short.

Procedure 5.2 — *Eliminating Glare on VDTs*

Purpose of this procedure

The purpose of this procedure is to determine whether employees are having problems with glare on their video display terminals (VDTs). Glare on VDTs can cause eyestrain and reduce an employee's ability to perform work.

When to use this procedure

This procedure should be performed for every employee who works at a workstation and uses a video display terminal. Also perform this procedure if you notice glare on employees' VDTs. Employees who are experiencing problems with glare should have their workstations assessed before those who are not experiencing problems.

Terms you may not know

Glare Unwanted reflected light on a VDT.
Glare hood A device that fits over the top of the monitor and projects out over the top of the screen to prevent offending light from striking the screen. Glare hoods work like the bill of a baseball cap.
Glare screen A device that fits in front of the monitor to reduce reflected light.

Before you start

Before you begin this procedure, you should perform Procedure 5.1. By doing so, you will satisfy the prerequisites for this procedure. You do not need a worksheet for this brief procedure.

What to do

The checklist for this procedure (Exhibit 5.2A) is very simple, but very important. Glare can hinder the ability of an employee to perform any task requiring the use of a VDT.

Example of procedure use

Ernie, a data entry clerk, had complained to Eleanor, his boss, that he was experiencing glare on his VDT. Eleanor recognized that this was an ergonomic problem and began going down the list of possible solutions. Placing the VDT at a ninety-degree angle to the window did not work. Placing dark blinds over the windows reduced the amount of natural light in the room to an unacceptable point. The only solution that worked was installing a glare screen. After, the glare screen was installed, Eleanor made sure that Ernie adjusted the brightness and the contrast of the VDT until he could see the characters clearly on the screen.

Exhibit 5.2A. Checklist for Eliminating Glare on VDTs.

Step	Criteria	Yes	No
1.	Is the employee experiencing glare on his or her VDT?	☐	☐

If yes, eliminate the glare by one of the following methods:

- Place the monitor screen at a 90° angle to windows or outside sources of light.

- Place dark blinds over windows. (This solution has a drawback in that some people like to look out the windows from time to time when they work. Thus this solution could cause other problems.)

- Find the offending light and partially block it (see Figure 5.2A). (Note that this solution may interfere with your fire protection system. Check with your fire protection engineer before you adopt this solution.)

- Purchase a glare screen to place over the monitor screen. Glare screens that are glass/optical–grade plastic and that use a polarizing filter appear to give better results than do the cloth screens, which must be cleaned frequently to prevent dust buildup. The light level and contrast on the monitor will need to be adjusted after a glare screen is installed.

- Purchase a glare hood that fits over the top of the monitor. Be careful that the hood does not cover the ventilation holes on top of the monitor. (In at least one case, a homemade hood that blocked the ventilation holes of the VDT has caused a fire.)

How to Do Step

Ask the employee about glare during the employee interview. Employees who have a severe problem with glare will readily let you know. You can also assess glare on a VDT by direct observation; that is, sit in the employee's chair and see for yourself. However, the first method is more accurate because your eye level may be higher or may be lower than the employee's and you may not see the screen as he or she does.

Figure 5.2A. Blocking a Light to Eliminate Glare.

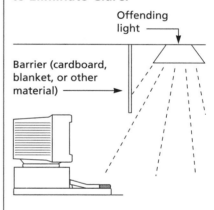

CHAPTER 6

Making Follow-Up Adjustments

Introduction

The procedure in this chapter shows you how and when to perform needed follow-ups to ergonomic assessments and adjustments, in order to ensure that the workplace is still ergonomically correct.

Procedure	When to Use	Page
6.1. Conducting Follow-Up Assessments	Routinely, to follow-up on ergonomic assessments and ensure that adjustments were appropriate and remain functional	130

What are the results of the procedure in this chapter?

The result of this procedure is a workforce that is more happy with management, because following up with employees proves that the company cares about them. If only the initial assessment is conducted, employees get the feeling that this is just another program that will go away after a few weeks. Follow-ups show that the company is committed to a healthy work environment and workforce. Follow-ups also continue the improvement the initial assessment started, because further problems can be detected and corrected.

| Procedure 6.1 | *Making Follow-Up Adjustments* |

Purpose of this procedure

Over time, tasks change, new technologies are added to the workplace, and workstations get out of adjustment. Therefore, it is important to conduct follow-ups. Follow-ups tell you whether the employee is still having the same problems or is having new ones. From the point of view of encouraging sound ergonomic practices, the worst thing that can happen is that a workstation adjusted to correct one problem winds up causing another. The employee can become very unhappy and tell fellow employees that this ergonomic stuff does not work. Therefore following up with employees helps you ensure that they are not having additional problems, and it shows them that you really do care about them.

When to use this procedure

This procedure should be performed after you have made any ergonomic intervention. Follow-ups need to be conducted at the following intervals to be effective:

- Two weeks after the initial assessment
- Six weeks after the initial assessment
- Yearly thereafter

Before you start

Before you begin your follow-up assessment, complete the following steps:

1. Obtain copies of the worksheets and notes you completed when you conducted the original intervention. This material will help you recall what was originally done, and suggest how you should structure your follow-up interview.

2. Obtain a photocopy of Worksheet B.3, How to Interview an Employee, for each employee whom you will reassess.

You do not need a worksheet for the follow-up procedure itself.

What to do

Complete the two steps in the checklist in Exhibit 6.1A.

Exhibit 6.1A. Making Follow-Up Adjustments.

Step	Assessment Checklist	Yes	No	How to Do Step
1.	Have the changes that were made in the initial adjustment affected the employee? If yes, find out whether the changes have been beneficial or not. If they have not been beneficial, repeat the appropriate assessment procedure to find a new solution.	☐	☐	Use Procedure 2.3 to conduct interviews with the employees on whom you are following up. Focus the interview on those areas that were changed as a result of the previous assessment.
2.	Has the employee experienced any other problems or does the employee want some other area of the workplace assessed? If yes, perform the appropriate procedures to find solutions to the new areas of concern.	☐	☐	Conduct any new or repeated procedures just as you would in an initial assessment, in order to ensure that all the relevant areas are covered.

Example of procedure use

Bill used procedures 3.1 and 4.1 to perform an ergonomic assessment of Erik's office. He subsequently recommended numerous changes, including a new desk and chair and the addition of task lighting. Bill adjusted the new furniture to Erik's needs when it arrived several days after the initial assessment. Two weeks later, Bill's tickler file reminded him that he needed to conduct a follow-up assessment. He made arrangements with both Erik and Erik's manager. He obtained copies of the original checklists and blank copies of the procedures. During the follow-up, he found that Erik's keyboard needed adjusting and that he was storing materials under his desk. Bill adjusted the keyboard and reminded Erik of the problems associated with storing materials in this manner. Bill documented these findings on the checklist and reported to Erik's manager. He made a note in his tickler file to conduct another follow-up in four weeks.

TECHNIQUES IN ACTION

Overview

What is this section about?

Chapter Seven. This chapter presents a case study that illustrates how the procedures in this book can be used to improve performance within a company. The procedures demonstrated in this chapter are 2.1: Reviewing Injury and Illness; 2.2: How to Interview a Manager; 2.3: How to Interview an Employee; 2.4: Organizing an Ergonomic Assessment; 3.1: Assessing a Sitting Workstation with VDT; 4.1: Assessing Workplace Layout; 4.2: Assessing Tasks Requiring Repetitive Motions of the Upper Extremities; 5.1: Assessing Lighting and Viewing Distance; 5.2: Eliminating Glare on VDTs; and 6.1: Making Follow-Up Adjustments.

How is this section organized?

CHAPTER 7

Restoring Lost Productivity: Case Study of the Springfield Loan Office

---

Introduction

This case study is intended to show you why managers or others charged with improving performance and productivity should consider ergonomic problems as a potential source of employees' productivity and performance difficulties. The study also illustrates in some detail how you should go about applying ergonomic assessment procedures and how your completed worksheets for those procedures might look.

Case Study

John Thomas was a human performance technologist for Mid-West Mortgage (MWM), a mortgage loan company with thirty-five offices in three states. His responsibilities included the evaluation of tasks and recommending changes to the task or to the training the employee received. The Springfield office of MWM had been in operation for three years and had nine staff members: a receptionist, two administrative assistants, three loan officers, a chief loan processor, an assistant loan processor, and an office manager. Officially, the office manager was the head of the office and all others reported to her.

John was asked to travel to the Springfield office to determine why in its third year it had not been processing loan forms as quickly as it had done over the previous two years. When John arrived, he introduced himself to Mary Smith, the office manager, and explained why he was there and his goals for the trip. Mary said that she had been told that he would visit and that she was willing to help him in any way she could. He then asked her a series of open-ended questions about the office employees' experience, training, and qualifications; about changes to office staff; and about the office atmosphere in general. He stressed that he was particularly interested in the loan processors since this was where the performance problem seemed to be located.

As Mary answered the questions, she described how Bob Kelf, the former chief loan processor, had recently become a loan officer and how Laura Baker had taken his place. Mary went on to say that Laura had been quite capable as the assistant loan processor before MWM promoted her, but at present, Mary said, she was disappointed. She knew Laura could do the job and she saw that Laura had done a good job in the position for the first few weeks, but now Laura was having problems. Her work output had decreased, she was taking a lot of sick time for nonspecific neck and shoulder pain, and she even appeared to be avoiding her office. Mary would find Laura working anywhere but in her office. Mary also said that Laura had received all the company training offered for her position and had even attended a special short course on loan processing at her own expense.

John then asked Mary why Mr. Kelf had become a loan officer, because that job was in a lower pay grade than the chief loan processor's job. Mary replied that he had developed a neck problem and had to find a job that did not require as much computer use.

From this interview, John felt that it was not the task or the level of employee ability that was resulting in the performance problem. Instead, he thought that maybe it was a problem with workplace design. He based his assumption on several factors:

- Laura had been a good performer until changing jobs.
- Laura's performance in the new job was good at first but was now becoming worse.
- Laura was taking sick time for musculoskeletal problems.
- Laura did not like working in her new office.
- The former person in that job had to change jobs because he had experienced neck problems.

John decided that he would conduct an ergonomic assessment of the chief loan processor's office to determine if there were ergonomic problems in the areas of posture, activities, or environment.

Performance of Procedure 1.1

John began the assessment by performing Procedure 2.1, Reviewing Injury or Illness Statistics. First he explained to Mary his intention of performing an ergonomic assessment, and when he found that Mary was not familiar with ergonomics, he explained the concept to her. He then explained that the first step of this procedure was to obtain a copy of the organization's OSHA 200 Form. Mary said she kept the office copy of this form but that it was blank because the Springfield office had had no occupational injuries requiring a physician's care. John asked about Bob's neck, and Mary replied that she did not think it was occupational because he had gone to his own physician. John then asked if the office maintained any other injury or illness statistics, and Mary said no. John completed the worksheet for Procedure 2.1 and noted that no recordable musculoskeletal injuries had occurred at the facility.

Performance of Procedure 2.2

At this point John decided to go right into the second part of the ergonomic assessment process, which is to interview the workplace manager more thoroughly using Procedure 2.2, How to Interview a Manager. Since John had previously explained the purpose of the assessment, he did not need to perform this preliminary step again. As he interviewed Mary in her office, he obtained several items of necessary information. See Exhibit 7.1 for a copy of John's completed worksheet. The outcome of this procedure showed that Mary knew of two cases of musculoskeletal problems in the office but had not connected them to workplace design. It was evident that the employees had complained of the workplace design, glare on video display terminals (VDTs), and lack of adequate space. Mary explained that the Springfield office had a limited budget and could not buy new equipment, so John asked Mary to calculate the cost of Laura's sick time. When Mary added it up, it came to $1,200 over the previous five months.

Performance of Procedure 2.3

John then made arrangements with Mary to interview both Bob and Laura. He also made arrangements to use the break room as an interview room. Getting the manager's cooperation and finding a comfortable place for the interview are prerequisites of Procedure 2.3, How to Interview an Employee. John interviewed each employee individually, using Worksheet B.2. The results of the interview with Bob showed that, as Mary had reported, he had experienced neck problems after working as the chief loan processor for eighteen months. At that point, he had decided to go back to being a loan officer. Bob thought that his problem was caused by using the computer for long periods of time, during which he had to crane his neck to see the monitor. He felt that if the monitor could have been lowered his neck would not have hurt, but the office manager had told him there was no budget to buy a new desk. After he returned to being a loan officer, his neck stopped bothering him.

Laura's interview revealed similar information. Laura was six inches shorter than Bob, and she said she had to crane her neck even more than Bob did to see the monitor.

Performance of Procedure 2.4

After conducting the three interviews, John sat down with the worksheet from Procedure 2.4, Organizing an Ergonomic Assessment, and the completed interview worksheets, and began to organize the rest of the ergonomic assessment. From this exercise, he determined that he needed to assess only the ergonomics of the loan processing office, and he made arrangements with Mary so that he could perform this assessment. Exhibit 7.2 shows his completed worksheet for Procedure 2.4.

Performance of Procedure 3.1

To start Procedure 3.1, Assessing a Sitting Workstation with VDT, John asked Laura to sit at her computer workstation in her normal posture. Using Figure 3.1A (see page 60) and Worksheet D.1 as his guides, John determined that Laura's VDT was too high, her wrists were not straight, and her elbow joint was bent at an angle less than 70 degrees. John's completed worksheet is shown in Exhibit 7.3. At first, John could not adjust the workstation, but he found that the top shelf on which the VDT sat could be removed, which lowered the VDT. However, the VDT was now too low, so he had to buy a VDT stand to put the VDT at the correct height for Laura. Laura's chair was adjustable, so to correct her arm position, John raised her chair. After the chair was raised, Laura's elbow joint was bent at a 90-degree angle, but her knee joint was now bent at an angle greater than 110 degrees, and her feet were dangling, unable to reach the floor. To correct this new problem John also showed Laura how to adjust her chair and explained the importance of shifting posture from time to time. The total cost for adjusting the workstation came to $85.

Performance of Procedure 4.1

John began Procedure 4.1, Assessing Workplace Layout, by asking Laura to sit in her chair and just stretch out her arms. It was immediately obvious she could not. Boxes of papers and filing cabinets were in the way. John noted this on the worksheet; then he asked Laura just to do her job for a while so he could watch her activities. During this time, John was performing step 2 of the procedure, which was to determine if the employee was working in her optimal reach envelope. After making his observations, John developed the link analysis shown in Figure 7.1.

This analysis showed that Laura performed twenty motions per hour into file cabinet B and five motions per hour into file cabinet A. All her motions into the file cabinets were outside her normal reach envelope. When John asked if there was a reason the filing cabinets were arranged so that cabinet A was closer to the desk than B, Laura replied that they were arranged that way when she began her job and she had not changed the arrangement. Since Mary was close at hand, John suggested that the three of them rearrange the office. They arranged the file cabinets so that all the important files were placed in cabinet A, and they moved the desk and cabinet A closer together, as depicted in Figure 7.2, so that the cabinet and the desk were within Laura's normal reach envelope.

The entry into the cubicle was a forty-four-inch-wide opening without a door and that width proved to be adequate for Laura's activities.

Figure 7.1. Link Analysis Chart for Laura's Job.

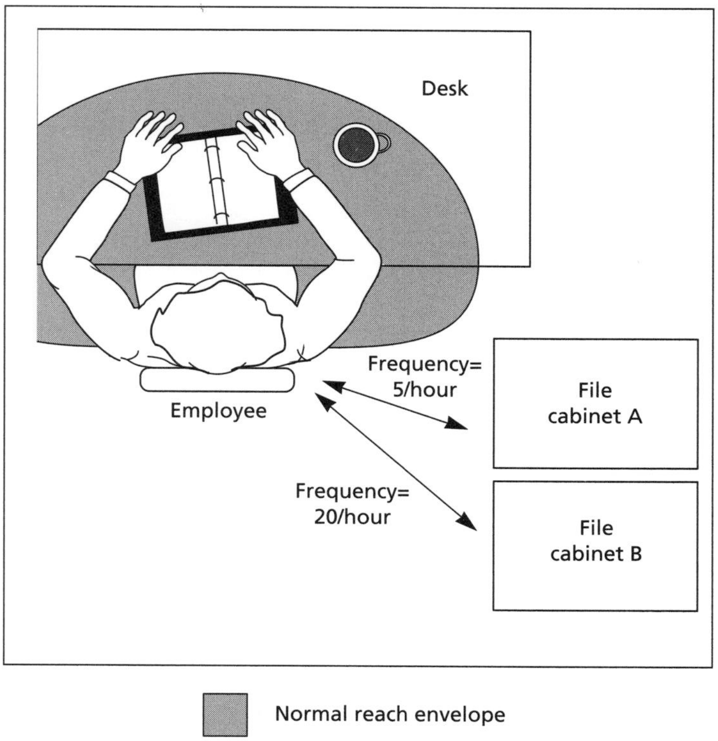

Normal reach envelope

Performance of Procedure 4.2

John next evaluated Laura's wrist postures when she typed and when she assembled the loan packets. Using Procedure 4.2, Assessing Tasks Requiring Repetitive Motions of the Upper Extremities, John found that Laura's wrist postures were neutral when she was typing, but deviated when she assembled the loan packets. John next estimated the number of wrist motions she made per hour when she assembled packets. He observed that she assembled ten packets per hour and deviated her wrists thirteen times per packet, for a total of 130 deviations per hour. He also noted that she only performed this task for two hours per day. From this data, John determined that this task was probably not an ergonomic problem. However, he did recommend that Laura consult a physical therapist for some stretching exercises to use when she took her breaks, to help alleviate fatigue. John also recommended to Mary that she conduct a training session on the causes of cumulative trauma disorders for her staff so they would know the risk factors and could better avoid them.

Figure 7.2. Office Rearrangement Based on Link Analysis.

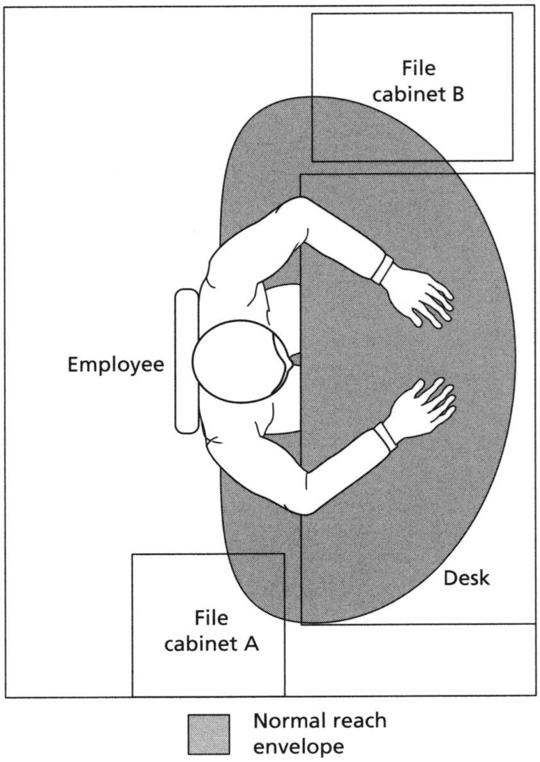

Normal reach
envelope

**Performance of
Procedure 5.1**

John's next task was to determine if there was adequate lighting and the viewing distance was proper. Using Procedure 5.1, Assessing Lighting and Viewing Distance, he determined that there were two locations at which Laura performed visual tasks: the part of her desk on which she proofread the loan packets and her computer monitor. When he used a light meter to measure the light in the area Laura used to proof the loan packet, the light level was 44 footcandles, but Table 5.1A showed that the lighting requirement for reading very poorly reproduced material was 93 to 186 footcandles. John recommended task lighting for this area. The light level in the computer monitor area was 40 footcandles, which was adequate.

John next measured the distance from Laura's eyes to the loan packet proofing area. The distance was ten inches and the distance recommended in Table 5.1B for such a visually demanding task was ten to fourteen inches, therefore John determined the ten-inch viewing distance to be adequate. He also measured the distance from Laura's eyes to the VDT and found the distance to be adequate.

Performance of Procedure 5.2

After correcting the workplace lighting, John moved on to Procedure 5.2, Eliminating Glare on VDTs. He asked Laura if she was having any problems with glare, and she said she had experienced glare, but since they had rearranged her office, she did not know if it would still be a problem. When John asked her to sit at the workstation to see if there was any glare on the VDT, she found there was definitely glare; it was so bad she could not see important parts of the screen. John first recommended to Mary that they place dark blinds over the windows when Laura was using her computer, but Mary thought that this would be a problem because the employees liked the natural light. John next suggested that Laura should try a glare screen, and Mary agreed to this strategy. John made sure to inform both Laura and Mary that the brightness level of the VDT would probably need to be increased and the contrast adjusted after the screen had been installed. The cost of the glare screen was $120.

Performance of Procedure 6.1

John had made arrangements with Mary to return in two weeks to follow-up the changes he had made in Laura's workplace. During the follow-up, he found that Laura had not had any more neck problems and had taken no sick time. John made arrangements to follow-up again in four weeks. At the second follow-up, he found no further problems.

Results of the procedures

John determined that the cost of the footrest, VDT stand, and glare screen was $205. He had spent four hours of his time on the assessment, which cost the company $100. The total cost of $305, however, was considerably less than Laura's sick time had cost to date and was far less than a CTD case's average cost, which is approximately $10,000. In addition, the Springfield office's loan processing speed returned to an efficient level of performance. (The fact that Bob Kelf, introduced on page 133, went on to find another job as chief loan processor reveals the high level of discomfort he had at this workplace.)

Exhibit 7.1. Completed Worksheet B.1 for a Manager Interview.

Evaluator: _____ John Thomas _____   Date: _____ May _____

Department or organizational unit being evaluated: ___ Springfield Office _____

Manager's name: ___ Mary Smith _____

Step	Interview Checklist	Yes	No
1.	Determine and then describe the types of tasks the employees perform:		
	Office tasks		
	Typing	☑	☐
	Filing	☑	☐
	Letter stuffing	☑	☐
	Proofreading	☑	☐
	Photocopying	☑	☐
	Bench work with light repair and assembly		
	Placing circuit boards in computers	☐	☑
	Handling objects weighing less than twenty pounds	☐	☑
	Using primarily the hands and wrists to perform the motions in the assembly or repair	☐	☑
	Working in a fast food restaurant	☐	☑
	Bench work with heavy assembly or repair		
	Assembling objects weighing over twenty pounds	☐	☑
	Using the elbows and shoulders to perform the motions used in the assembly or repair	☐	☑
	Light lifting: lifting only a few containers in a day		
	Heavy lifting: lifting numerous containers in a day	☐	☑
	Manufacturing: operating milling machines, lathes, tools weighing over twenty pounds	☐	☑
	Heavy service industries		
	Servicing cars, trucks, and buses	☐	☑
	Working in cafeterias	☐	☑
	Working in laundries	☐	☑
	Description: Reviewing loan application forms on a personal computer and determining what other information is needed on the form. Proofing the loan package, which involves comparing the loan form against the documents submitted by the applicants. The documents are then assembled in a packet. The packet is copied and one copy is placed in a file. The second copy is mailed to the main office.		
2.	What types of workstation are used in the workplace:		
	Standing	☐	☐
	Sitting	☑	☐
	With VDT	☑	☐

Step	Interview Checklist	Yes	No
3.	Ask the manager to describe the workstation or workplace. Description: *An 8-foot × 10-foot cubicle with fluorescent lighting. One outside window without blinds. The office appeared well lit. The office was crowded. There were two filing cabinets in the office.*		
4.	Ask the manager to discuss any employee complaints of pain, discomfort, or other problems, and determine the body parts where employees are experiencing pain or discomfort:		
	Neck	☑	☐
	Shoulder	☑	☐
	Upper back	☐	☑
	Lower back	☐	☑
	Elbow/forearm	☐	☑
	Hand/wrist	☑	☐
	Fingers	☐	☑
	Thigh/knee	☐	☑
	Lower leg	☐	☑
	Ankle/foot	☐	☑
5.	Ask the manager to list all specific complaints the employees might be having with:		
	Lighting	☐	☑
	Glare on computer screens	☑	☐
	Noise	☐	☑
	Thermal environment	☐	☑
	Vibration	☐	☑
	Lack of adequate space	☑	☐
	Workplace furniture (benches, chairs, desks) that causes postural stress	☑	☐
6.	Have there been any recent changes in the workplace that might have affected the employees' ability to perform work?	☑	☐
	If yes, determine what has changed recently. Description: *Laura was new to the position. Bill recently left the position.*		

Exhibit 7.1. (Continued)

Step	Interview Checklist	Yes	No
7.	Do any employees use sick time for back pain or other musculoskeletal problems?	☑	☐
	If yes, then list the problems here. Description: _Employee said she was having neck, shoulder, and wrist problems but thought they were due to stress of the new position._		
8.	Determine what the manager feels are the reasons for the employees' complaints and list the reasons here. Description: _Stress of new job._		
9.	Tour the facility with the manager in order to get a feel for the magnitude of task, get initial impressions of the types of problems employees may be having, and give employees the opportunity to begin to know you. Determine the following from your tour:		
	Is the workplace clean and orderly?	☑	☐
	Does the lighting appear adequate?	☑	☐
	Does the workplace feel too hot or cold?	☐	☑
	Does the workplace sound too noisy?	☐	☑
	Are employees exposed to vibration?	☐	☑

Summary of Findings: _Employees were experiencing neck, shoulder, and wrist problems indicative of workplace design problems._

Exhibit 7.2. Completed Worksheet C.1 for Organizing an Ergonomic Assessment.

Evaluator: _____John Thomas_____ Date: __May__

Department or organizational unit being evaluated: __Springfield Office__

Step	Organization Checklist	Yes	No
1.	Check that you have data in all the areas in the following list. Seek help from an ergonomic specialist if you have a problem in an area marked with an asterisk.		
	Postures		
	Standing	☐	☑
	Sitting	☑	☐
	With VDT	☑	☐
	Activities		
	Office tasks		
	Typing	☑	☐
	Filing	☑	☐
	Letter stuffing	☑	☐
	Proofreading	☑	☐
	Photocopying	☑	☐
	Bench work with light repair and assembly		
	Placing circuit boards in computers	☐	☑
	Handling objects weighing less than twenty pounds	☐	☑
	Using primarily the hands and wrists to perform the motions in the assembly or repair	☐	☑
	Working in a fast food restaurant	☐	☑
	*Bench work with heavy assembly or repair		
	Assembling objects weighing over twenty pounds	☐	☑
	Using the elbows and shoulders to perform the motions used in the assembly or repair	☐	☑
	Light lifting: lifting only a few containers in a day	☐	☑
	*Heavy lifting: lifting numerous containers in a day	☐	☑
	*Manufacturing: operating milling machines, lathes, tools weighing over twenty pounds	☐	☑
	*Heavy service industries		
	Servicing cars, trucks, and buses	☐	☑
	Working in cafeterias	☐	☑
	Working in laundries	☐	☑

Exhibit 7.2. (Continued)

Step	Organization Checklist	Yes	No
	Specific activities problems		
	Lack of adequate space	☑	☐
	Problems with workplace layout	☑	☐
	Many hand and upper-extremity activities	☑	☐
	Environment		
	Lighting	☑	☐
	Glare on computer screens	☑	☐
	*Noise	☐	☑
	*Thermal environment	☐	☑
	*Vibration	☐	☑
2.	Judging from your initial assessment of the problem, does an ergonomic specialist need to be consulted?	☐	☑
	If yes, for which parts of the assessment is a specialist needed? Description: _____		

3. Describe the types of workplaces and all the problems the ergonomic assessment will examine. Description: *Sitting computer workstation. This assessment will focus on the adjustment of the workstation to the employee. The lighting in the work area will be assessed and a determination made concerning any glare problems. The arrangement of the workstation will also be assessed.*

4. Use the data you have collected and Table 2.4A to decide which procedures need to be performed for which workstations. List the workstations here and mark the numbers of the procedures to be performed.

Workstations	Procedures
Loan processing office	**3.1** 3.2 **3.3** 3.4 3.5 3.6 3.7 **4.1** **4.2 4.3** 4.4 **5.1 5.2**

Step	Organization Checklist	Yes	No
5.	Schedule your assessments with the manager and the employees to ensure that everyone will be available and that the employees will be performing the tasks to be assessed at the scheduled time.		

Date for the assessment: <u>Today</u> Time: <u>Now</u>
Areas to be assessed: <u>Loan processing office.</u>

_____

_____

Summary of Findings: <u>*Procedure 3.3 will not be performed if it is possible to adjust Laura to her*</u>
<u>*workstation.*</u>

_____

_____

_____

_____

_____

_____

_____

_____

_____

Exhibit 7.3. Completed Worksheet D.1 for Assessing a Sitting Workstation with VDT.

Evaluator: _____ John Thomas _____ Date: _____ May _____

Department or organizational unit being evaluated: __ Springfield Office _____

Step	Assessment Checklist	Yes	No
1.	Is the elbow joint bent at approximately a 90° angle while the employee is using the keyboard (the angle can range from 70° to 110°)?	☐	☑
	If no, adjust the chair height and/or keyboard height. If these cannot be adjusted, try a different chair and/or desk. Most companies have a storage area that is a good source of old furniture. Consider buying a different chair or desk if there is no other way to achieve the correct elbow angle.		
2.	Is the hip joint bent at approximately a 90° angle (the angle can range from 90° to 110°)?	☑	☐
	If no, adjust the chair height or try a different chair.		
3.	Are the ears, shoulders, and hips lined up vertically (the head can be tipped slightly forward at a comfortable angle of 5° to 10°)?	☐	☑
	If no, then adjust the chair height, the angle of the backrest, the viewing distance to the VDT (see Procedure 5.1), or the keyboard height.		
4.	Are the wrists straight?	☐	☑
	If no, adjust the chair height or the keyboard height. Try a different chair and/or desk if the workstation cannot be properly adjusted. Also, consider using a wrist rest (see Procedure 4.3).		
5.	Is a mouse used at the workstation?	☐	☑
	If yes, perform steps 5a, 5b, and 5c.		
5a.	Is the elbow bent at a 90° angle while the employee is using the mouse (the angle can range from 70° to 110°)?	☐	☐
	If no, move the mouse closer to the person. An arm support can also be used (see Procedure 4.3).		
5b.	Is the upper arm close to the body?	☐	☐
	If no, then move the mouse closer to the person.		
5c.	Is the wrist deviated?	☐	☐
	If yes, adjust the height of the mouse and/or use a wrist rest (see Procedure 4.3).		

Step	Assessment Checklist	Yes	No
6.	Are the employee's knees bent at a 90° angle (the angle can range from 70° to 110°)? If no, adjust the chair height or try a different chair.	☐	☑
7.	Are the feet supported? If no, give the employee a footrest because at this point the workstation has been adjusted for the employee's elbows, hips, wrists, and knees.	☐	☑
8.	Is the VDT at the proper viewing distance (approximately the employee's arm length)? If no, adjust the distance of the monitor from the employee's eyes, moving the monitor forward or back until it is positioned correctly. A monitor arm can help you achieve the correct position.	☑	☐
9.	Is there adequate thigh and leg clearance? If no, try a desk with a thinner top to provide more leg clearance. Remove items stored underneath the desk.	☑	☐
10.	Is the part of the screen the employee uses most within the normal cone of vision, which is +5° (above the horizontal axis) to −30° (below the horizontal axis)? If no, adjust the height of the VDT. This can be done by removing the monitor base if the monitor is too high or adding a monitor base if the monitor is too low. A monitor arm can also be used to raise or lower the VDT.	☐	☑
11.	Are there any sharp edges pressing into the employee? If yes, pad the items that are causing problems with light foam rubber or remove them.	☐	☑
12.	Return to step 1 and repeat steps 1 through 11 to ensure that the body alignment is still correct in every aspect.		

Summary of Findings: _Laura was adjusted to her workstation by removing the top shelf of the desk and adjusting her chair. Therefore, it is not necessary to perform Procedure 3.3._

_____

_____

_____

RESOURCES

Overview

What is this section about?

Resources A, B, C, D, and E. These resources contain blank worksheets for the procedures in Section Two. You are encouraged to photocopy these worksheets and use them as procedure guides in your own ergonomic assessments.

Resource F. This resource is a glossary of all the special terms and acronyms that appear in this book.

How is this section organized?

Resource A: Injury and Illness Statistics Review Worksheet

WORKSHEET A.1 Checklist for Reviewing Injury and Illness Statistics

Evaluator: _____ Date: _____

Department or organizational unit being evaluated: _____

Note: Before you begin this procedure obtain a copy of the OSHA Form 200 for the organization being evaluated.

Step	Review Checklist	Yes	No
1.	Are there any musculoskeletal injuries or illnesses listed in column F of the OSHA Form 200?	☐	☐
	If yes, note the injury or illness, department, and occupation of the employee below.		

Injury or Illness	Department	Occupation
_____	_____	_____
_____	_____	_____
_____	_____	_____
_____	_____	_____
_____	_____	_____

Step	Review Checklist	Yes	No
2.	Did the injuries or illnesses require days away from work or days of restricted activity? Note: Days away from work are normally more serious than days of restricted activity.	☐	☐
	If yes, determine how many days away from work or days of restricted work there were for each musculoskeletal injury or illness. To determine total days add columns 4, 5, 11, and 12 on OSHA Form 200: _____ days.		
3.	Determine the total number of employees who work in each of the departments and perform the occupations that appear on the OSHA form.		

Occupation	Number of Employees
_____	_____
_____	_____
_____	_____
_____	_____
_____	_____

Resource A   (Continued)

WORKSHEET A.1   (Continued)

Step	Review Checklist	Yes No
4.	Divide the total number of employees who perform the occupation by the total number of injuries and illnesses that involve days away from work or days of restricted activity, and enter the result using the spaces provided. The result estimates musculoskeletal injury and illness rate. Repeat the procedure for injuries and illnesses that do not involve restricted days or days away from work.	

(Number of employees who perform task)/(Number of Injuries) = Rate

Occupation: _____
(_____ employees)/(_____ injuries) = _____ rate

Occupation: _____
(_____ employees)/(_____ injuries) = _____ rate

Occupation: _____
(_____ employees)/(_____ injuries) = _____ rate

Occupation: _____
(_____ employees)/(_____ injuries) = _____ rate

Occupation: _____
(_____ employees)/(_____ injuries) = _____ rate

Summary of Findings:

_____

_____

_____

_____

_____

_____

_____

Resource B: Interview Worksheets

WORKSHEET B.1 Checklist for Interviewing a Manager

Evaluator: _____ Date: _____

Department or organizational unit being evaluated: _____

Manager's name: _____

Step	Interview Checklist	Yes	No
1.	Determine and then describe the types of tasks the employees perform:		
	Office tasks		
	Typing	☐	☐
	Filing	☐	☐
	Letter stuffing	☐	☐
	Proofreading	☐	☐
	Photocopying	☐	☐
	Bench work with light repair and assembly		
	Placing circuit boards in computers	☐	☐
	Handling objects weighing less than twenty pounds	☐	☐
	Using primarily the hands and wrists to perform the motions in the assembly or repair	☐	☐
	Working in a fast food restaurant	☐	☐
	Bench work with heavy assembly or repair		
	Assembling objects weighing over twenty pounds	☐	☐
	Using the elbows and shoulders to perform the motions used in the assembly or repair	☐	☐
	Light lifting: lifting only a few containers in a day	☐	☐
	Heavy lifting: lifting numerous containers in a day	☐	☐
	Manufacturing: operating milling machines, lathes, tools weighing over twenty pounds	☐	☐
	Heavy service industries		
	Servicing cars, trucks, and buses	☐	☐
	Working in cafeterias	☐	☐
	Working in laundries	☐	☐

Description: _____

_____

_____

_____

_____

_____

Resource B *(Continued)*

WORKSHEET B.1 **(Continued)**

Step	Interview Checklist	Yes	No
2.	What types of workstations are used in the workplace:		
	Standing	☐	☐
	Sitting	☐	☐
	With VDT	☐	☐
3.	Ask the manager to describe the workstation and/or workplace. Description:		

_____

_____

_____

_____

_____

_____

_____

_____

_____

_____

Step	Interview Checklist	Yes	No
4.	Ask the manager to discuss any employee complaints of pain, discomfort, or other problems, and determine the body parts where employees are experiencing pain or discomfort:		
	Neck	☐	☐
	Shoulder	☐	☐
	Upper back	☐	☐
	Lower back	☐	☐
	Elbow/forearm	☐	☐
	Hand/wrist	☐	☐
	Fingers	☐	☐
	Thigh/knee	☐	☐
	Lower leg	☐	☐
	Ankle/foot	☐	☐

Step	Interview Checklist	Yes	No
5.	Ask the manager to list all specific complaints the employees might be having with the following environmental factors:		
	Lighting	☐	☐
	Glare on computer screens	☐	☐
	Noise	☐	☐
	Thermal environment	☐	☐
	Vibration	☐	☐
	Lack of adequate space	☐	☐
	Workplace furniture (benches, chairs, desks) that causes postural stress	☐	☐
6.	Have there been any recent changes in the workplace that might have affected employees' ability to perform work?	☐	☐

If yes, determine what has changed recently. Description: _____

_____

_____

_____

_____

Step	Interview Checklist	Yes	No
7.	Do any employees use sick time for back pain or other musculoskeletal problems?	☐	☐

If yes, list the problems here. Description: _____

_____

_____

_____

_____

8.   Determine what the manager feels are the reasons for the employees' complaints and list the reasons here. Description: _____

_____

_____

_____

_____

Resource B   (Continued)

WORKSHEET B.1   (Continued)

Step	Interview Checklist	Yes	No
9.	Tour the facility with the manager in order to get a feel for the magnitude of the task, get initial impressions of the types of problems employees may be having, and give employees the opportunity to begin to know you. Determine the following from your tour:	☐	☐
	Is the workplace clean and orderly?		
	Does the lighting appear adequate?	☐	☐
	Does the workplace feel too hot or cold?	☐	☐
	Does the workplace sound too noisy?	☐	☐
	Are employees exposed to vibration?	☐	☐

Summary of Findings:

_____

_____

_____

_____

_____

_____

_____

_____

_____

**WORKSHEET B.2 Checklist for Interviewing an Employee
(Complete a separate sheet for each employee)**

Employee designator: _____

Evaluator: _____ Date: _____

Department or organizational unit being evaluated: _____

Step	Interview Checklist	Yes	No
1.	Is the employee experiencing any musculoskeletal problems?	☐	☐
	If no, go to step 2.		
	If yes, perform steps 1a, 1b, 1c, 1d, and 1e.		
1a.	Ask the employee to indicate his or her problem areas on the front and back body diagrams included in this worksheet.		
1b.	Determine the type of physical symptoms the employee is having, including aching, burning, color loss, cramping, numbness ("asleep"), pain, stiffness, swelling, tingling, weakness, or other symptoms. Enter this information as the "problem type" in the appropriate box on the body diagram.		
1c.	Ask the employee to indicate the relative severity of the problem on a scale from 1 to 10, with 1 being a minimal problem and 10 being unbearable. Enter this rating as the "severity" in the appropriate box on the body diagram.		
1d.	Has the employee sought medical attention for the problem either from the company physician or a private physician?	☐	☐
	If no, encourage the employee to see the company physician, or a private physician if there is no company physician.		
	If yes, ask what the doctor said.		
1e.	Does the employee have an idea about what is causing the problem?	☐	☐
	If yes, note the employee's idea here and use it as the starting point of the assessment. Description: _____ _____		

Step	Interview Checklist	Yes	No
2.	Does the employee have trouble reaching needed items in the workplace?	☐	☐
3.	Does the employee have any difficulty attaining and staying in the postures required by the workplace?	☐	☐
4.	Does the employee like the way his or her workstation is arranged?	☐	☐
5.	Does the employee feel cramped in his or her workplace?	☐	☐
6.	Can the employee attain a full range of motion in his or her workplace?	☐	☐
7.	Does the employee have to lift items in his or her workplace?	☐	☐
8.	Does the employee have problems with any of the following:		
	Lighting levels	☐	☐
	Glare on a computer screen	☐	☐
	Noise	☐	☐
	Temperature of the workplace	☐	☐
	Vibration	☐	☐
9.	Has the employee had training on any of the following:		
	The causes of cumulative trauma disorders	☐	☐
	The causes of back injuries	☐	☐
	The benefits of microbreaks	☐	☐
	How to perform stretching exercises	☐	☐
	How to adjust his or her workstation and/or chair	☐	☐
	If the answer to any of these items in step 9 is yes, does the employee feel the training was adequate?	☐	☐

Summary of Findings:

_____

_____

_____

_____

_____

_____

Front Body Diagram to Identify Musculoskeletal Problems.

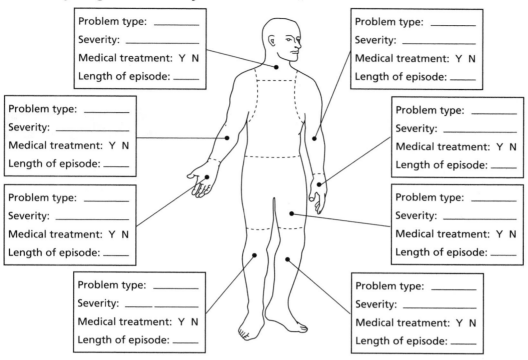

Problem type: _____
Severity: _____
Medical treatment: Y N
Length of episode: _____

Problem type: _____
Severity: _____
Medical treatment: Y N
Length of episode: _____

Problem type: _____
Severity: _____
Medical treatment: Y N
Length of episode: _____

Problem type: _____
Severity: _____
Medical treatment: Y N
Length of episode: _____

Problem type: _____
Severity: _____
Medical treatment: Y N
Length of episode: _____

Problem type: _____
Severity: _____ _____
Medical treatment: Y N
Length of episode: _____

Problem type: _____
Severity: _____
Medical treatment: Y N
Length of episode: _____

Back Body Diagram to Identify Musculoskeletal Problems.

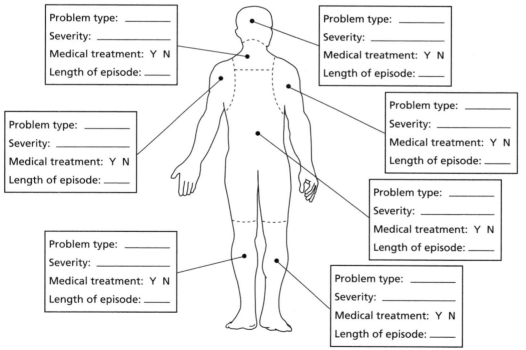

Problem type: _____
Severity: _____
Medical treatment: Y N
Length of episode: _____

Problem type: _____
Severity: _____
Medical treatment: Y N
Length of episode: _____

Problem type: _____
Severity: _____
Medical treatment: Y N
Length of episode: _____

Problem type: _____
Severity: _____
Medical treatment: Y N
Length of episode: _____

Problem type: _____
Severity: _____
Medical treatment: Y N
Length of episode: _____

Problem type: _____
Severity: _____
Medical treatment: Y N
Length of episode: _____

Resource C: Worksheet for Organizing the Ergonomic Assessment

WORKSHEET C.1 Checklist for Organizing the Ergonomic Assessment

Evaluator: _____   Date: _____

Department or organizational unit being evaluated: _____

Step	Organization Checklist	Yes	No
1.	Check that you have data in all the areas in the following list. Seek help from an ergonomic specialist if you have a problem in an area marked with an asterisk.		
	Postures		
	Standing	☐	☐
	Sitting	☐	☐
	With VDT	☐	☐
	Activities		
	Office tasks		
	Typing	☐	☐
	Filing	☐	☐
	Letter stuffing	☐	☐
	Proofreading	☐	☐
	Photocopying	☐	☐
	Bench work with light repair and assembly		
	Placing circuit boards in computers	☐	☐
	Handling objects weighing less than twenty pounds	☐	☐
	Using primarily the hands and wrists to perform the motions in the assembly or repair	☐	☐
	Working in a fast food restaurant	☐	☐
	*Bench work with heavy assembly or repair		
	Assembling objects weighing over twenty pounds	☐	☐
	Using the elbows and shoulders to perform the motions used in the assembly or repair	☐	☐
	Light lifting: lifting only a few containers in a day	☐	☐
	*Heavy lifting: lifting numerous containers in a day	☐	☐
	*Manufacturing: operating milling machines, lathes, tools weighing over twenty pounds	☐	☐
	*Heavy service industries		
	Servicing cars, trucks, and buses	☐	☐
	Working in cafeterias	☐	☐
	Working in laundries	☐	☐
	Specific activities problems		
	Lack of adequate space	☐	☐
	Problems with workplace layout	☐	☐
	Many hand and upper-extremity activities	☐	☐

	Environment		
	Lighting	☐	☐
	Glare on computer screens	☐	☐
	*Noise	☐	☐
	*Thermal environment	☐	☐
	*Vibration	☐	☐

2. Judging from your initial assessment of the problems, does an ergonomic specialist need to be consulted? ☐ ☐

If yes, for which parts of the assessment is a specialist needed? Description:

_____

_____

_____

_____

_____

3. Describe the types of workplaces and all the problems the ergonomic assessment will examine: _____

_____

_____

_____

_____

_____

_____

_____

_____

Resource C   (Continued)

WORKSHEET C.1   (Continued)

Step	Organization Checklist	Yes No

4. Use the data you have collected and Table 2.4A to decide which procedures to perform for which workstations. List the workstations here and mark the numbers of the procedures to be performed.

Workstations	Procedures
_____	3.1 3.2 3.3 3.4 3.5 3.6 3.7 4.1 4.2 4.3 4.4 5.1 5.2
_____	3.1 3.2 3.3 3.4 3.5 3.6 3.7 4.1 4.2 4.3 4.4 5.1 5.2
_____	3.1 3.2 3.3 3.4 3.5 3.6 3.7 4.1 4.2 4.3 4.4 5.1 5.2
_____	3.1 3.2 3.3 3.4 3.5 3.6 3.7 4.1 4.2 4.3 4.4 5.1 5.2
_____	3.1 3.2 3.3 3.4 3.5 3.6 3.7 4.1 4.2 4.3 4.4 5.1 5.2

5. Schedule your assessments with the manager and the employees to ensure that everyone will be available and that the employees will be performing the tasks to be assessed at the scheduled time.

Date for the assessment: _____   Time: _____

Areas to be assessed: _____

_____

_____

_____

_____

Summary of Findings:

_____

_____

_____

_____

_____

_____

_____

_____

_____

Resource D: Assessment and Evaluation Worksheets

WORKSHEET D.1 Checklist for Assessing a Sitting Workstation with VDT (Refer to Figure 3.1A for Workstation Illustration)

Evaluator: _____ Date: _____

Department or organizational unit being evaluated: _____

Step	Assessment Checklist	Yes	No
1.	Is the elbow joint bent at approximately a 90° angle while the employee is using the keyboard (the angle can range from 70° to 110°)?	☐	☐
	If no, adjust the chair height and/or keyboard height. If they cannot be adjusted, try a different chair and/or desk. Most companies have a storage area that is a good source of old furniture. Consider buying a different chair or desk if there is no other way to achieve the correct elbow angle.		
2.	Is the hip joint bent at approximately a 90° angle (the angle can range from 90° to 110°)?	☐	☐
	If no, adjust the chair height or try a different chair.		
3.	Are the ears, shoulders, and hips lined up vertically (the head can be tipped slightly forward at a comfortable angle of 5° to 10°)?	☐	☐
	If no, adjust the chair height, the angle of the backrest, the viewing distance to the VDT (see Procedure 5.1), or the keyboard height.		
4.	Are the wrists straight?	☐	☐
	If no, adjust the chair height or the keyboard height. Try a different chair and/or desk if the workstation cannot be properly adjusted. Also, consider using a wrist rest (see Procedure 4.3).		
5.	Is a mouse used at the workstation?	☐	☐
	If yes, perform steps 5a, 5b, and 5c.		
5a.	Is the elbow bent at a 90° angle while the employee is using the mouse (the angle can range from 70° to 110°)?	☐	☐
	If no, move the mouse closer to the person. An arm support can also be used (see Procedure 4.3).		

Resource D   (Continued)

WORKSHEET D.1   (Continued)

Step	Assessment Checklist	Yes	No
5b.	Is the upper arm close to the body?	☐	☐
	If no, move the mouse closer to the person.		
5c.	Is the wrist deviated?	☐	☐
	If yes, adjust the height of the mouse and/or use a wrist rest (see Procedure 4.3).		
6.	Are the knees bent at a 90° angle (the angle can range from 70° to 110°)?	☐	☐
	If no adjust the chair height or try a different chair.		
7.	Are the feet supported?	☐	☐
	If no, give the employee a footrest because at this point the workstation has been adjusted for the employee's elbows, hips, wrists, and knees.		
8.	Is the VDT at the proper viewing distance (approximately the employee's arm length)?	☐	☐
	If no, adjust the distance of the monitor from the employee's eyes, moving the monitor forward or back until it is positioned correctly. A monitor arm can help you achieve the correct position.		
9.	Is there adequate thigh and leg clearance?	☐	☐
	If no, try a desk with a thinner top to provide more leg clearance. Remove items stored underneath the desk.		
10.	Is the part of the screen the employee uses most within the normal cone of vision, which is +5° (above the horizontal axis) to −30° (below the horizontal axis)?	☐	☐
	If no, adjust the height of the VDT. This can be done by removing the monitor base if the monitor is too high or adding a monitor base if the monitor is too low. A monitor arm can also be used to raise or lower the VDT.		
11.	Are any sharp edges pressing into the employee?	☐	☐
	If yes, pad the items that are causing problems with light foam rubber or remove them.		
12.	Return to step 1 and repeat steps 1 through 11 to ensure that the body alignment is still correct in every aspect.		

Summary of Findings:

_____

_____

_____

_____

_____

_____

_____

_____

Resource D   (Continued)

WORKSHEET D.2 Checklist for Assessing a Sitting Workstation Without VDT (Refer to Figure 3.2A on page 65 for Workstation Illustration)

Evaluator: _____   Date: _____

Department or organizational unit being evaluated: _____

Step	Assessment Checklist	Yes	No
1.	Is the workpiece at the correct height for the type of task (6 inches above elbow height for fine work like proofing documents or inspecting small parts, 4 inches above elbow height for precision work like mechanical assembly, same height as elbow for writing or light assembly, 4 inches below elbow height for coarse or medium work like packaging)?	☐	☐
	If no, adjust the chair height or the height of the workpiece. You can adjust the height of the workpiece by using a document holder for papers or a fixture for mechanical work. Also, you can raise or lower the workbench or desk by adding height to the legs or cutting them shorter.		
2.	Are the knees bent at a 90° angle (the angle can range from 70° to 110°)?	☐	☐
	If no, adjust the chair height or try a different chair.		
3.	Are the ears, shoulders, and hips lined up vertically (the head can be tipped slightly forward at a comfortable angle of 5° to 10°)?	☐	☐
	If no, adjust the chair height, the angle of the backrest, or the viewing distance to the workpiece (see Procedure 5.1).		
4.	Are the shoulders relaxed?	☐	☐
	If no, adjust the chair height or the workpiece height.		
5.	Is there adequate thigh and leg clearance?	☐	☐
	If no, try a desk with a thinner top that provides more leg clearance. Remove the items stored underneath the desk.		

Step	Assessment Checklist	Yes	No
6.	Are the feet supported?	☐	☐
	If no, the employee needs a footrest because at this point the workstation has been adjusted for the employee's elbows, hips, wrists, and knees.		
7.	Is the hip joint bent at approximately a 90° angle (the angle can range from 90° to 100°)?	☐	☐
	If no, adjust the chair height or try a different chair.		
8.	Are any sharp edges pressing into the employee?	☐	☐
	If yes, pad the items that are causing problems with light foam rubber or remove them.		
9.	Return to step 1 and repeat steps 1 through 8 to ensure that the body alignment is still correct in every aspect.		

Summary of Findings:

_____

_____

_____

_____

_____

_____

_____

_____

Resource D   *(Continued)*

WORKSHEET D.3 Checklist for Assessing a Standing Workstation with VDT (Refer to Figure 3.5A on page 82 for Workstation Illustration)

Evaluator: _____   Date: _____

Department or organizational unit being evaluated: _____

Step	Assessment Checklist	Yes	No
1.	Is the elbow joint bent at approximately a 90° angle while the employee is using the keyboard and the upper arm is pointing down (the angle can range from 70° to 110°)?	☐	☐
	If no, adjust the keyboard height. If the keyboard height cannot be adjusted, try a different desk. Most companies have a storage area that is a good source of old furniture. Consider buying a new desk if there is no other way to achieve the correct elbow angle.		
2.	Are the wrists straight?	☐	☐
	If no, adjust the height of the keyboard. Try a different desk if the workstation cannot be properly adjusted. Also, consider using a wrist rest (see Procedure 4.3).		
3.	Are the ears, shoulders, and hips lined up vertically (the head can be tipped slightly forward at a comfortable angle of 5° to 10°)?	☐	☐
	If no, adjust the keyboard height or the viewing distance to the VDT (see Procedure 5.1).		
4.	Is the VDT at the proper viewing distance (approximately the employee's arm length)?	☐	☐
	If no, adjust the distance of the monitor from the employee's eyes. Move the monitor forward or back until it is positioned correctly. A monitor arm can help you achieve the correct position.		
5.	Is the part of the screen the employee uses most within the normal cone of vision, which is +5° (above the horizontal axis) to −30° (below the horizontal axis)?	☐	☐
	If no, adjust the height of the VDT by removing the monitor base if the monitor is too high or adding a monitor base on if the monitor is too low. A monitor arm can also be used to raise or lower the VDT.		
6.	Is there adequate leg room?	☐	☐
	If no, remove the obstacles that prevent the employee from attaining a desirable standing posture.		

Step	Assessment Checklist	Yes	No
7.	Can the employee elevate one foot?	☐	☐
	If no, consider installing a rail or finding a small wooden or metal box for this purpose.		
8.	Are there any sharp edges pressing into the employee?	☐	☐
	If yes, pad the items that are causing problems with light foam rubber or remove them.		
9.	Is a mouse used at the workstation?	☐	☐
	If yes, perform steps 9a, 9b, and 9c.		
9a.	Is the elbow bent at a 90° angle (the angle can range from 70° to 110°)?	☐	☐
	If no, move the mouse closer to the person. An arm support can also be used (see Procedure 4.3).		
9b.	Is the upper arm close to the body?	☐	☐
	If no, move the mouse closer to the person.		
9c.	Is the wrist deviated?	☐	☐
	If yes, adjust the height of the mouse and/or use a wrist rest (see Procedure 4.3).		
10.	Return to step 1 and repeat steps 1 through 9 to ensure that the body alignment is still correct in every aspect.		

Summary of Findings:

_____

_____

_____

_____

_____

_____

_____

_____

_____

Resource D   (Continued)

WORKSHEET D.4 Checklist for Assessing a Standing Workstation Without VDT (Refer to Figure 3.6A on page 88 for Workstation Illustration)

Evaluator: _____   Date: _____

Department or organizational unit being evaluated: _____

Step	Assessment Checklist	Yes	No
1.	Is the workpiece at the correct height for type of task (4 inches above elbow height for precision work with supported elbows, same height as elbow for light assembly work, 4 inches below elbow height for heavy work)?	☐	☐
	If no, adjust the height of the workpiece by using a document holder for papers or a fixture for mechanical work. Also, you can raise or lower the workbench or desk by adding height to the legs or cutting them shorter.		
2.	Are the ears, shoulders, and hips lined up vertically (the head can be tipped slightly forward at a comfortable angle of 5° to 10°)?	☐	☐
	If no, adjust the workpiece height. A physical obstacle such as items stored under the workstation may also be hindering the employee from attaining a desirable posture.		
3.	Can the employee elevate one foot?	☐	☐
	If no, consider installing a rail or finding a small wooden or metal box for this purpose.		
4.	Is there adequate leg room?	☐	☐
	If no, remove the obstacles that prevent the employee from attaining a desirable standing posture.		
5.	Are there any sharp edges pressing into the employee?	☐	☐
	If yes, pad the items that are causing problems with light foam rubber or remove them.		
6.	Return to step 1 and repeat steps 1 through 5 to ensure that the body alignment is still correct in every aspect.		

Summary of Findings:

_____

_____

_____

_____

WORKSHEET D.5 Checklist for Assessing Workplace Layout (Refer to Figures 4.1A, 4.1B, 4.1C, and 4.1D on pages 98–100 for Related Illustrations)

Evaluator: _____ Date: _____

Department or organizational unit being evaluated: _____

Step	Assessment Checklist	Yes	No
1.	Does the employee have adequate room to attain a full range of motion?	☐	☐
	If no, rearrange the workplace to allow the employee a full range of motion.		
2.	Is the workstation arranged so the objects the employee uses most are closest to him or her and within his or her reach envelope?	☐	☐
	If no, rearrange the layout so items used are optimally arranged given the employee's reach envelope.		
3.	Do the workplace doors swing in the direction of travel?	☐	☐
	If no, change the direction of the swing of the door or make the door bi-directional. In most cases, this can be done easily with the help of building maintenance personnel.		
4.	Are the doors or openings wide enough?	☐	☐
	If no, widen the door or opening or institute an administrative control, such as controlling how employees can use the door or opening.		

Summary of Findings:

_____

_____

_____

_____

_____

_____

_____

_____

Resource D (Continued)

WORKSHEET D.6 Checklist for Assessing Tasks Requiring Repetitive Motion of the Upper Extremities

Evaluator: _____ Date: _____

Department or organizational unit being evaluated: _____

Step	Assessment Checklist	Yes	No
1.	Is the employee observed performing a task with the wrist or an upper extremity deviated?	☐	☐
	If yes, modify the task using any of the following methods:		
	• Change the tool used to perform the task. Figure 4.2B shows how a different tool can change wrist postures. The ergonomic design philosophy is *bend the tool, not the human.*		
	• Adjust the workstation (see the procedures in Chapter Three).		
	• Use a wrist rest to keep the wrist in a neutral posture for typing tasks (see Procedure 4.3).		
	• Use a jig or fixture to position the workpiece comfortably rather than allow the employee to deviate his or her posture to work on the item.		
2.	Is the task highly repetitive?	☐	☐
	If yes, reduce the number of repetitions by automating the task or by alternating the tasks the employee performs. For example, have employee A perform task A for a 2-hour period and then alternate tasks with employee B who is performing task B. This only works, however, if the sets of motions required by tasks A and B are different. Or develop a matrix of tasks and their demands and schedule the tasks so that the employee does not perform like tasks sequentially. If you wish to determine cycle times of tasks consult an ergonomic expert.		
3.	Is the employee provided with enough rest breaks?	☐	☐
	If no, the employee should be encouraged to take a microbreak every 30 minutes and to perform stretching exercises during that break.		
4.	Has the employee been trained on the risk factors associated with CTDs?	☐	☐
	If no, then train the employee on the previous CTDs experienced in the company and the department, the four risk factors associated with CTDs, and the importance of reporting ergonomic problems to management. Training should be provided upon employment and annually thereafter.		

Summary of Findings:

_____

_____

_____

_____

_____

_____

_____

_____

Resource D   (Continued)

WORKSHEET D.7 Checklist for Assessing Tasks Requiring Lifting

Evaluator: _____ Date: _____

Department or organizational unit being evaluated: _____

Step	Assessment Checklist	Yes	No
1.	Weigh the container the employee is lifting: _____ pounds		
2.	Determine the approximate lift range (see Exhibit 4.4A and Figure 4.4A). (Use your judgment and choose the closest match.)		
	0 to 29 inches	☐	☐
	29 to 65 inches	☐	☐
	0 to 65 inches	☐	☐
3.	Compare the weight of the container to the weight limit for that range (see Exhibit 4.4A). Weight limit: _____ pounds		
4.	Is the employee lifting more than he or she should?		
	If yes, then mechanical means should be used or the weight of the container should be reduced.		
5.	Has the employee been trained about the hazards of improper lifting?	☐	☐
	If no, then train employee. Exhibit 4.4C shows the rules for lifting that should be included in a training program. Employees should also be informed about any lifting tasks that have resulted in employee injuries.		

Summary of Findings:

_____

_____

_____

_____

WORKSHEET D.8 Checklist for Assessing Lighting and Viewing Distance

Evaluator: _____ Date: _____

Department or organizational unit being evaluated: _____

Task title: _____

Step	Assessment Checklist	Yes	No
1.	What is current lighting level: _____ foot-candles _____ lux		
2.	What is the lighting level requirement for the task from (see Table 5.1A): _____ footcandles _____ lux		
3.	Compare the values found in steps 1 and 2. Are the lighting levels correct for the task? If no, supply more light to the task through such means as task lighting.	☐	☐
4.	What is current viewing distance: _____ inches		
5.	What is the viewing distance requirement for this task (see Table 5.1B): _____ inches		
6.	Compare the distances found in steps 4 and 5. Is the viewing distance correct for task? If no, then adjust the viewing distance by adjusting the workstation or the position of the work.	☐	☐

Summary of Findings:

_____

_____

_____

_____

_____

_____

_____

_____

Resource E: Furniture and Equipment Selection Worksheets

WORKSHEET E.1 Checklist for Selecting a Chair (Refer to Figure 3.3A on page 71 for Chair Illustrations)

Evaluator: _____ Date: _____

Department or organizational unit being evaluated: _____

Step	Selection Checklist	Yes	No
1.	Does the chair adjust up and down for a seat pan height of between 20 to 26 inches for workstations with footrests and 15.5 to 20 inches for workstations without footrests?	☐	☐
2.	Does the backrest have an adjustable inclination?	☐	☐
3.	Does the backrest latch at the desired inclination?	☐	☐
4.	Does the chair allow for forward and reclined sitting postures?	☐	☐
5.	Does the backrest rise 19 to 22 inches vertically above the seat surface?	☐	☐
6.	Is the backrest height adjustable?	☐	☐
7.	Is the upper part of the backrest slightly concave?	☐	☐
8.	Is the width of the backrest at least 13 to 14 inches?	☐	☐
9.	Does the backrest have a lumbar pad that provides support to the lumbar spine between the third vertebra and the sacrum, that is, at a height of 4 to 8 inches above the lowest point of the seat surface?	☐	☐
10.	Is the seat pan width at least 16 to 18 inches?	☐	☐
11.	Is the seat pan length at least 15 to 17 inches?	☐	☐
12.	Is the front of the seat pan rounded?	☐	☐
13.	Is the seat pan lightly padded (approximately 2 inches thick)?	☐	☐
14.	Does the material covering the chair prevent slipping and draw perspiration away from the body?	☐	☐
15.	Does the chair have a five-point base?	☐	☐
16.	If the chair has castors, do they lock?	☐	☐
17.	Can the chair be easily cleaned?	☐	☐

Step	Selection Checklist	Yes	No
18.	Does the employee feel the chair is acceptable?	☐	☐
19.	Can the employee adjust the chair easily?	☐	☐
20.	Can the employee make the adjustments without the potential for injury?	☐	☐
21.	How long is the chair's warranty? _____		
22.	What is the chair's cost? $_____		

Summary of Findings:

_____

_____

_____

_____

_____

_____

_____

_____

_____

Resource E (Continued)

WORKSHEET E.2 Checklist for Selecting a Sitting Workstation (Refer to Figures 3.4A and 3.4B on page 77 for Workstation Illustrations)

Evaluator: _____ Date: _____

Department or organizational unit being evaluated: _____

Step	Selection Checklist	Yes	No
1.	Does the workstation provide 26 inches of leg clearance?	☐	☐
2.	Is the work surface less than 2 inches thick?	☐	☐
3.	Is there approximately 8 inches of thigh clearance?	☐	☐
4.	Is the work surface height adjustable between 26 and 34 inches?	☐	☐
5.	Are there sharp edges that could press into the employee?	☐	☐
6.	Is a VDT to be used at this workstation? If no, go to step 9.	☐	☐
7.	Is the height of the keyboard home row adjustable from 22 to 28 inches?	☐	☐
8.	Does the workstation allow the VDT to be used within the viewing distance of the employee at the correct height?	☐	☐
9.	Does the employee accept the workstation?	☐	☐

Summary of Findings:

_____

_____

_____

_____

WORKSHEET E.3 Checklist for Selecting a Standing Workstation (Refer to Figures 3.7A and 3.7B on page 92 for Workstation Illustrations)

Evaluator: _____ Date: _____

Department or organizational unit being evaluated: _____

Step	Selection Checklist	Yes	No
1.	Does the workstation provide 20 inches of knee and foot clearance?	☐	☐
2.	Is the work surface height adjustable from 36 to 44 inches?	☐	☐
3.	Are there sharp edges that could press into the employee?	☐	☐
4.	Does the workstation have a foot rail for elevating one foot?	☐	☐
5.	Is a VDT to be used at this workstation? If no, go to step 8.	☐	☐
6.	Is the height of the keyboard home row adjustable from 36 to 44 inches?	☐	☐
7.	Does the workstation allow a VDT to be used within the employee's viewing distance and at the correct height for the employee?	☐	☐
8.	Does the employee accept the workstation?	☐	☐

Summary of Findings:

_____

_____

_____

_____

_____

_____

_____

_____

Resource F: Glossary

Abduction Movement of a limb away from the body's midline axis, for example, elevating the elbow or raising the arm away from the side.

Adduction Movement of a limb toward the body's midline axis, for example, bringing the arm down to the side.

Anthropometry The study of people in terms of their physical dimensions.

Arm support A device that typically attaches to the workstation or desk in order to support the forearm.

Biomechanics The application of mechanical principles, such as leverage and force, to the analysis of a body-part structure and movement.

Capacity The maximum ability of a person to perform under a given set of conditions.

Carpal tunnel syndrome Compression of the median nerve of the hand and wrist in the carpal tunnel, usually resulting in numbness in the fingers, pain, and loss of grip strength.

Compression force A force applied perpendicularly to a surface.

Cumulative trauma disorder (CTD) A class of musculoskeletal or neurological disorders associated with repetitive tasks in which forceful exertions of the fingers, wrist, hand, elbow, or shoulder are required.

de Quervain's syndrome A variety of tenosynovitis that occurs in the tendons of the thumb.

Deviated Not in a neutral posture.

Document stand A device that holds a document to be read.

Dynamic In motion.

Egress An exit.

Employee designator A way to identify an employee that may or may not be the employee's name, the designator may be a number, a letter, or a pseudonym.

Epicondylitis An irritation of the tendons attached to the epicondyle in the elbow.

Epidemiology The study of the causes and effects of illnesses and injuries.

Ergonomics An applied science that matches the demands of tasks to the capabilities and limitations of the individuals who perform the tasks.

Fatigue A reduction in performance ability due to physical or mental activity levels exceeding a person's capacity.

Fixture A device that holds a workpiece in a desired configuration. Traditionally, a fixture is attached to the workpiece with screws whereas a jig is attached to the workpiece with clamps.

Food calorie See *kilocalorie*.

Footcandle A U.S. measure of illumination. One foot-candle equals approximately ten lux.

Force Mass times acceleration.

Glare Unwanted reflected light on a VDT.

Glare hood A device that fits over the top of a monitor to prevent offending light from striking the screen.

Glare screen A device that fits in front of a monitor to reduce reflected light.

Illness A condition of poor health. Cumulative trauma disorders are usually classified as illnesses.

Illumination Amount of light falling on a surface.

Injury A physically undesirable condition due to an accident. Back problems are usually classified as injuries.

Jig A device that holds a workpiece in a desired configuration.

Kilocalorie (kcal) The amount of heat required to raise one kilogram of water one degree Celsius. One kcal equals one food calorie.

Life Safety Code A set of standards developed by the National Fire Protection Association to prevent people from being killed due to panic in the event of fire. These standards are also OSHA regulations.

Link analysis An analysis technique that determines physical associations between people and their workplaces.

Lost workday case A severe illness or injury that results in one or more days away from work.

Lux An SI measure of illumination.

Manual material handling The act of moving materials without machinery.

Maximum acceptable weight of lift Psychophysical measure of perceived lifting capacity.

Maximum heart rate Defined as 220 minus one's age. For example, the maximum heart rate of a thirty-six-year-old person is 184 (220 − 36 = 184).

Microbreak A very short rest break lasting around one minute and occurring every thirty minutes or so during the day.

Monitor arm A jointed arm-like device on which a computer monitor is placed to give it mobility.

Musculoskeletal Pertaining to the muscles, bones, and joints.

Neck tension An irritation of a group of muscles related to the neck.

NFPA National Fire Protection Association.

NIOSH National Institute for Occupational Safety and Health, a research institute of the U.S. Department of Health and Human Services. NIOSH provides research information to the Occupational Safety and Health Administration.

Normal cone of vision The field within which the eye can easily rotate to see objects.

Open-ended question A question that cannot be answered with just a yes or a no.

OSHA The Occupational Safety and Health Administration.

OSHA Form 200 The form that OSHA requires to be kept as a record of workplace injuries and illnesses.

Oxygen consumption The rate at which the body's tissues and cells use oxygen.

Palmar Flexion A wrist position in which the hand is flexed toward the palm.

PC Personal computer.

Perceived exertion A psychophysical measure of the amount of effort required for a given action or task.

Physical effort The use of muscles to accomplish a task.

Physical work capacity (PWC) The highest oxygen uptake an individual can attain during physical work.

Posture The relative arrangement of body parts, specifically the orientation of the limbs, trunk, and head during a work task.

Psychophysics A science concerned with perceived physical limits and the relationship between physical sensations and their physical stimuli.

Radial deviation Movement of the hand toward the thumb side.

Raynaud's syndrome A condition in which blood flow to the hand is reduced and the fingers feel cold.

Recordable injury or illness An injury or illness requiring a physician's care.

Recovery time Work periods when task demands are light or when rest is provided.

Restricted activity case An illness or injury so severe that the employee has to be assigned to other tasks because he or she cannot perform his or her normal job.

SI International System of units; the metric system.

Static work A work configuration that requires the employee to hold a stressful posture for a period of time. There is no exact period of time that the posture must be held in order to be called static. The determination is dependent on the muscles being used and the posture.

Stress Physiological, psychological, environmental, or mental effects that may produce fatigue or degrade a person's performance.

Task lighting Lighting provided close to the point of work.

Tendon Connective tissue that connects bone to muscle.

Tendon sheath A structure that surrounds tendons at certain locations in the body and that secretes synovial fluid, which allows easier movement of the tendon.

Tendinitis Inflammation of a tendon.

Tenosynovitis Inflammation of a tendon sheath.

Thoracic outlet syndrome (TOS) A compression of the nerves and blood vessels between the collarbone and first and second ribs.

Trigger finger A variety of tendinitis in which a tendon becomes nearly locked.

Ulnar Deviation Movement of the hand toward the little finger side.

VDT Video display terminal, or computer monitor.

Viewing distance Distance from the eye to the object being viewed.

Work physiology The science concerned with the organs and systems that supply energy to move the body or parts of the body.

Workpiece Any item an employee is working on.

Workplace The physical area in which a person performs job activities.

Workstation A workplace that is included in a production system or on a piece of manufacturing equipment.

Wrist rest A device, usually a bar made of firm foam rubber, placed under the wrists to keep them in a neutral posture.

References

American National Standards Institute/Human Factors Society. *American National Standard for Human Factors Engineering of Visual Display Terminal Workstations.* Santa Monica, Calif.: Human Factors Society, 1988.

American Optometric Association. *VDT User's Guide to Better Vision.* 1992. St. Louis, Mo.: American Optometric Association, 1992.

Andersson, G. B. J. "Epidemiological Aspects of Low Back Pain in Industry." *Spine,* 1981, *6,* 54–60.

Andersson, G. B. J., and Ortengren, R. "Lumbar Disc Pressure and Myoelectric Back Muscle Activity During Sitting: Two Studies on an Office Chair." Scandinavian Journal of Rehabilitation Medicine, 1974, *3,* 115–121.

Astrand, P. O., and Rodahl, K. *Textbook of Work Physiology.* (3rd ed.) New York: McGraw-Hill, 1986.

Ayoub, M. M. "Workplace Design and Posture." *Human Factors,* 1973, *15*(3), 265–268.

Ayoub, M. M., and others. *Determination and Modeling of Lifting Capacity.* Final report. U.S. Department of Health Education Welfare/National Association for Occupational Safety and Health, 1978.

Ayoub, M. M., and Mital, A. *Manual Materials Handling.* Bristol, Pa.: Taylor and Francis, 1989.

Ayoub, M. M., and others. *Manual Materials Handling in Unusual Positions: Phase IV, Final Report.* Lubbock, Tex.: Texas Tech University, 1988.

Barnes, R. M. *Motion and Time Study: Design and Measurement of Work.* (7th ed.) New York: Wiley, 1980.

Brogmus, G. E., and Marko, R. "The Proportion of Cumulative Trauma Disorders of the Upper Extremities in U.S. Industry." *Proceedings of the Human Factors Society 36th Annual Meeting,* Atlanta, Ga., 1992.

Bullock, D. *Training Consultant's Memo, 1*(1), pp. 3–8. Simpson Ville, Md.: D. Bullock, 1981.

Chaffin, D. B., and Andersson, G. B. J. *Occupational Biomechanics.* New York: Wiley, 1984.

Current, R. N., Williams, T. H., and Freidel, F. *American History: A Survey.* (4th ed.) Vol. I: *To 1877.* New York: Knopf, 1975.

Diffrient, N., Tilley, A., and Harmon, D. *Humanscale.* Cambridge, Mass.: MIT Press, 1991.

Donkin, S. W. *Sitting on the Job.* Boston: Houghton Mifflin, 1989.

Emanuel, J., Mills, S., and Bennett, J. "In Search of a Better Handle." Proceedings of the Symposium: Human Factors and Industrial Design in Consumer Products. Medford, Mass: Tufts University, 1980.

Finnish Institute of Occupational Health. *Ergonomic Workplace Analysis.* Helsinki, Finland. Publication Office, Institute of Occupational Health, 1989.

Foreman, T. K., Baxter, C. E., and Troup, J. D. "Ratings of Acceptable Load and Maximal Isometric Lifting Strengths: The Effects of Repetition." *Ergonomics,* 1984, *27,* 1283–1288.

Garg, A., and Ayoub, M. M. "What Criteria Exist for Determining How Much Load Can Be Lifted Safely?" *Human Factors.* 1980, *22,* 475–486.

Garrett, A. *Interviewing. The Principles and Methods.* New York: Family Service Organization of America, 1972.

Gemme, G. "Symptomatology and Diagnostic Methods in the Hand-Arm Vibration Syndrome." *Scandinavian Journal of Work Environmental Health,* 1987, *13*(4), 271–388.

Grandjean, E. *Ergonomics in Computerized Offices.* Bristol, Pa.: Taylor and Francis, 1987.

Grandjean, E. *Fitting the Task to the Man.* (4th ed.) Bristol, Pa.: Taylor and Francis, 1990.

Guyton, A. C. *Physiology of the Human Body.* (8th ed.) Philadelphia, Pa.: Saunders College Publishing, 1990.

Hafez, H. A. "An Investigation of Biomechanical, Physiological, and Environmental Heat Stresses Associated with Manual Lifting in Hot Environments." Unpublished doctoral dissertation. Texas Tech University, 1984.

Houghton, F. C., and Yagloglou, S. P. "Determination of the Comfort Zone." *Journal of the American Society of Heating and Ventilation Engineers,* 1923, *29,* 515–536.

Jiang, B. C. "Psychophysical Capacity Modeling of Individual and Combined Manual Materials Handling Activities." Unpublished doctoral dissertation. Texas Tech University, 1984.

Karwawski, W. "A Fuzzy Sets Model on Interaction Between Stresses Involved in Manual Lifting Tasks." Unpublished doctoral dissertation. Texas Tech University, 1982.

Klein, B. P., Roger, M. A., Jensen, R. C., and Sanderson, L. M. "Assessment of Workers' Compensation Claims for Back Sprain/Strain." *Journal of Occupational Medicine,* 1984, *26,* 443–448.

Kroemer, K. H. E. "Avoiding Cumulative Trauma Disorders in Shops and Offices." *American Industrial Hygiene Association Journal,* 1992, *53*(9), 596–604.

Kroemer, K. H. E., Kroemer, H. J., and Kroemer-Elbert, K. E. *Engineering Physiology,* New York: Van Nostrand Reinhold, 1990.

Lathrop, J. K. *Life Safety Code Handbook.* (5th ed.) National Fire Protection Association, Quincy, Mass.: Batterymarch Park, 1991.

Leamon, T. Discussion during M. M. Ayoub's Occupational Ergonomic Symposium, Lubbock, Tex., 1993.

McArdle, W. D., Katch, F. I., and Katch, V. L. *Exercise Physiology,* Philadelphia, Pa.: Lea and Febiger, 1986.

McCormick, E. J., and Sanders, M. S. *Human Factors in Engineering Design.* (5th ed.) New York: McGraw-Hill, 1982.

Meister, D. *Behavioral Analysis and Measurement Methods.* New York: Wiley, 1985.

Mital, A. "Effects of Task Variable Interaction in Lifting and Lowering." Unpublished doctoral dissertation, Texas Tech University, 1980.

Mital, A. "The Psychophysical Approach in Manual Lifting: A Verification Study." *Human Factors,* 1983, *25,* 485–491.

National Safety Council, *Accident Prevention Manual for Industrial Operations.* Chicago, Ill.: National Safety Council, 1981.

National Safety Council, *Accident Facts.* Chicago, Ill.: National Safety Council, 1990.

National Institute of Occupational Safety and Health (NIOSH). *The Industrial Environment: Its Evaluation and Control.* Washington, D.C.: U.S. Government Printing Office, 1973.

National Institute of Occupational Safety and Health (NIOSH). *Work Practice Guide for Manual Lifting.* Technical Report. Cincinnati, Ohio: U.S. Government Printing Office, 1981.

National Society for Performance and Instruction. *Handbook of Human Performance and Technology: A Comprehensive Guide for Analyzing and Solving Performance Problems in Organizations.* San Francisco: Jossey-Bass, 1992.

Occupational Safety and Health Administration. OSHA 29 CFR 1910, *General Industry Standards,* 1989.

Ostrom, L. T. "The Effects of Rigid Container Height and Shape on Maximum Acceptable Weight of Lift." Unpublished doctoral dissertation, Texas Tech University, 1988.

Ostrom, L. T., Gilbert, B. G., and Wilhelmsen, C. A. *Summary of the Ergonomic Assessments of Selected EG&G Idaho Work Places* (EGG-2652), Idaho Falls, Idaho: 1991.

Pheasant, S. T. *Bodyspace: Anthropometry, Ergonomics and Design.* Bristol, Pa.: Taylor and Francis, 1986.

Putz-Anderson, V. *Cumulative Trauma Disorders: A Manual for Musculoskeletal Diseases of the Upper Limbs.* Bristol, Pa.: Taylor and Francis, 1988.

Putz-Anderson, V., and Waters, T. "Revisions in NIOSH Guide to Manual Lifting." Paper presented at a National Strategy for Occupational Musculoskeletal Injury Prevention Conference, Ann Arbor, Mich., 1991.

Rodahl, K. *The Physiology of Work.* Bristol, Pa.: Taylor and Francis, 1989.

Rodgers, S. H. *Ergonomic Design for People at Work.* Belmont, Calif.: Lifetime Learning Publications, 1983.

Roebuck, J. A., Kroemer, K. H. E., and Thomson, W. G. *Engineering Anthropometry Methods.* New York: Wiley, 1975.

Romero, H. A., Ostrom, L. T., and Wilhelmsen, C. A. "What Difference Can the Data Make." *Proceedings of the Human Factors Society 37th Annual Meeting,* Seattle, Wash., 1993.

Rossett, A. "Analysis of Human Performance Problems." In H. D. Stolovitch and E. J. Keeps (eds.), *Handbook of Human Performance Technology.* San Francisco: Jossey-Bass, 1992.

Rummler, G. A., and Brache, A. P. "Transforming Organizations Through Human Performance Technology." In H. D. Stolovich and E. J. Keeps (eds.), *Handbook of Human Performance Technology.* San Francisco: Jossey-Bass, 1992.

Rummler, G. A., and Brache, A. P. *Improving Performance: How to Manage the White Space on the Organization Chart.* San Francisco: Jossey-Bass, 1990.

Scholander, P. F., Walters, V., Hook, R., and Irving, L., "Body Insulation of Some Arctic and Tropical Mammals and Birds." *Biology Bulletin,* 1950, *99,* 250.

Smith, P., and Kearny, L. *Creating Workplaces Where People Can Think.* San Francisco: Jossey-Bass, 1994.

Snook, S. H. "The Design of Manual Materials Handling Tasks." *Ergonomics,* 1978, *21,* 963–985.

Snook, S. H. "Low Back Pain in Industry." Proceedings of the Symposium on Idiopathic Low Back Pain, St. Louis, 1982, pp. 23–38.

Stevens, S. S. "The Psychophysics of Sensory Function." *American Scientist,* 1960, *48,* 226–253.

Stevens, S. S. *Psychophysics: Introduction to Its Perceptual, Neural, and Social Prospects.* New York: Wiley, 1975.

Stolovich, H. D., and Keeps, E. J. "What is Human Performance Technology?" In H. D. Stolovich and E. J. Keeps (eds.), *Handbook of Human Performance Technology.* San Francisco: Jossey-Bass, 1992.

U.S. Air Force. *U.S. Air Force Guide to Mishap Investigation.* AFP 127-1, Vol I. Washington, D.C.: U.S. Government Printing Office, 1987.

Van Cott, H. P., and Kincade, R. G. *Human Engineering Guide to Equipment Design.* New York: McGraw-Hill, 1972.

Webster's Encyclopedic Dictionary of the English Language. Chicago: The English Language Institute of America, 1975.

Index

E

Egress, 97

Employee. *See* Interview of employee; Workers

Environment, 26; design criteria with, 29; guidelines on variables in, 27; lighting in, 26–27; noise in, 27; thermal, 27; vibration in, 27

Epicondylitis (tennis elbow), 6, 25

Epidemiology, 24–25

Ergonomic assessment, organizing, 49; for case study, 138, 145–147; checklist for, 50–51; procedure decision table for, 52–54; worksheet for, 145–147, 162–164

Ergonomic gadgets, assessing, 110–112; checklist for, 112; example of, 112

Ergonomics, 3; principles of, 8–10

F

Fatigue, 16, 23

Finnish Institute of Occupational Health, 123

Fixture, definition of, 64, 87, 103

Follow-up adjustments, making, 130; for case study, 141; checklist for, 131; example of, 131

Footcandle, 121

Force(s): biomechanical, 22; as descriptor of task, 22; posture and, acting on back, 12; reduction of, to reduce injury, 25

Foreman, T. K., 24

Freidel, F., 3

G

Garg, A., 23

Garrett, A., 36

Gemme, G., 27

Glare, 126; eliminating, on VDTs, 126–127, 141

Glare hood, 126

Glare screen, 126

Grandjean, E., 3, 8, 16, 17, 57, 60, 70, 82, 120

Grip postures, 106

Guyton, A. C., 23

H

Hafez, H. A., 27

Harmon, D., 18

Houghton, F. C., 24

Human Performance Technology (HPT), xi–xii; views of work of, xii–xiii

I

Illness, 37

Illumination, 121

Injury, 37. *See also* Musculoskeletal injuries

Injury and illness statistics review, 37–39; for case study, 137; checklist for, 40; example of, 39; OSHA Form 200 for, 37–39; worksheet for, 153–154

International System of Units, (SI), 121

Interview of employee, 45; for case study, 137; checklist for, 46–48; example of, 48; worksheet for, 159–161

Interview of manager, 41; for case study, 137, 142–144; checklist for, 42–44; example of, 44; worksheet for, 142–144, 155–158

J

Jensen, R. C., 7

Jiang, B. C., 24

Jig, 64, 87, 103

Job enrichment, 4

K

Karwowski, W., 24

Katch, F. I., 23

Katch, V. L., 23

Kearny, L., 26, 119, 120

Kinkade, R. G., 18, 21, 57

Klein, B. P., 7

Kroemer, K.H.E., 5, 7, 20

L

Lathrop, J. K., 97, 101

Leamon, T., 21

Repetitive motion syndromes, 5
Rest: as descriptor of task, 22; to reduce injury, 26; wrist, 59, 80, 110, 111. *See also* Microbreaks
Restricted activity case, 37
Rodahl, K., 22, 23, 96
Roebuck, J. A., 20
Roger, M. A., 7
Rogers, S. H., 57, 70, 120, 123
Romero, H. A., 20

S

Sanders, M. S., 24, 124
Sanderson, L. M., 7
Self-paced work, 24
Shoulder, posture for, 105
Sitting posture(s): anthropometric data for, 18; and chair design, 17; effect of workplace arrangement on, 14; equations for anthropometric data for, 20; varying, 16; at workstation with VDT, 60; at workstation without VDT, 65
Sitting workstation: criteria for, 77; good posture at, 60, 65
Sitting workstation, selecting, 76–77; checklist for, 78; example of, 79; worksheet for, 180
Sitting workstation with VDT, assessing, 58–60; for case study, 138, 148–149; checklist for, 61–63; example of, 60; worksheet for, 148–149, 165–167
Sitting workstation without VDT, assessing, 64–65; checklist for, 66–68; example of, 69; workstation for, 168–169
Smith, P., 26, 119, 120
Snook, S. H., 7, 24
Standardization, in production, 3–4
Standing posture: anthropometric data for, 19; equations for anthropometric data for, 20; and forces on back, 12; at workstation with VDT, 82; at workstation without VDT, 88
Standing workstation: criteria for, 92; good posture at, 82, 88

Standing workstation, selecting, 91–92; checklist for, 93; example of, 94; worksheet for, 181
Standing workstation with VDT, assessing, 80–82; checklist for, 83–85; example of, 86; worksheet for, 170–171
Standing workstation without VDT, assessing, 87–88; checklist for, 89–90; example of, 90; worksheet for, 172–173
Stevens, S. S., 24
Symptoms, diseases with similar, 5

T

Task lighting, 121, 125
Tasks: with cumulative trauma disorders, 25; design criteria with, 29; fitting, to individual worker, 8; pace of, 22; terms for describing, 22
Tasks requiring lifting, assessing, 113–114; checklist for, 115–116; example of, 117; worksheet for, 176
Tasks requiring repetition, assessing, 103–104; for case study, 139–140; checklist for, 107–109; example of, 104–106; worksheet for, 174–175
Taylor, F., 4
Temperature. *See* Thermal environment
Tendinitis, 6; shoulder, 25; wrist, 25
Tendon, 5
Tendon sheath, 5, 14
Tennis elbow. *See* Epicondylitis (tennis elbow)
Tenosynovitis, 6
Tension neck, 25
Thermal environment, 27
Thomson, W. G., 20
Thoracic outlet syndrome (TOS), 7, 25
Tilley, A., 18
Tools, and wrist posture, 106
Training: cost of, as measurable outcome, 28; limitations of, 10–11; and physical work capacity, 23
Trigger finger, 6
Troup, J. D., 24